Hi Ho Librario!

Hi Ho Librario!

Songs, Chants, and Stories
to Keep Kids Humming

By Judy Freeman

rockhill communications, Bala Cynwyd, PA

Published by RockHill Communications
www.webfeetguides.com
Copyright ©1997 Judy Freeman
All rights reserved.
Printed and bound in the United States
Second printing 2000.

Credits appear on p. viii.

A recording of songs, chants, and stories from *Hi Ho Librario!* is available on CD or audiocassette. Contact RockHill Communications, 14 Rock Hill Road, Bala Cynwyd, PA 19004; 1-888-ROCKHIL; 610-667-2040; 610-667-2291 (fax); info@rockhillcommunications.com.

Library of Congress Catalog Card Number: 97-80008

ISBN 1-890604-00-3
ISBN 1-890604-01-1 (with CD)
ISBN 1-890604-02-X (with audiotape)

ISBN 1-890604-00-3

9 781890 604004

Design by RockHill Communications
Music transcribed by Karen Beyer

To Izzy, of course,
who has heard every song
over and over,
even in his sleep.

Acknowledgments

Special thanks to

Catherine Barr, my editor, who not only thought this was a good idea, but sat through every take

The fabulous Wednesday Workshoppers at the Somerset County Library, the best children's book writers group in the universe

Louise Sherman for coming up with so many stellar songs over the years

Librarian buddies Cathy Darby, Renee Jackson, and Lois Farrah who made such on-target suggestions

All the swell librarians on LM_NET who kept me poring over interesting mail when I should've been writing

Producer Mike Testa for letting me fool around with all his great guitars, and Jim McClurken and Ernie Mazzarise for all the musical challenges

My students at Van Holten School in Bridgewater, NJ, for their love of a good song

Frank Vignola, former student, whose poem "Someone Ate the Teacher" is still one of my favorites

Kristen D'Allesandro and Allison Testa of Millington, NJ, and Kristen McClurken of Califon, NJ, for their expert chanting

My library assistant, Sharon Kalter, who always knows where the guitar picks are lurking

My musical family: sister Sharron Freeman, brother Richard Freeman, and parents Bob and Gladys Freeman

Credits

Every reasonable effort has been made to identify materials under copyright and to obtain appropriate permissions to reproduce such materials in this volume. If notified of omissions, the editor and publisher will make necessary corrections in future editions.

Page 64	"Ladies and Jellybeans." *Source:* New York State Historical Association Library, Jones Archive.
Pages 96–97	"Alligator Pie." From *Alligator Pie* (Macmillan of Canada, 1974). Copyright © 1974 Dennis Lee. With permission of the author.
Pages 119–120	"Henry My Son." Used by permission. See details page 120.

Illustrations

By students in Bridgewater, NJ
HILLSIDE INTERMEDIATE SCHOOL
Grade 5

Page 56	Brian Koenig	Page 103	Heather Linton	Page 123	Jennifer Yuan

EISENHOWER INTERMEDIATE SCHOOL
Grade 4
Page 91 Whitney Ryan

VAN HOLTEN PRIMARY SCHOOL
Grade 3

Page 28	Lucy Zhou	Page 62	Elizabeth Franchino	Page 63	Mark Kunsman
Page 64	Ted Lin	Page 70	Mike Sandford	Page 72	Jackie Cacciatore
Page 74	Lindsey Campanelli	Page 75	Cara Healey	Page 76	Lisa Wood
Page 78	Arjun Ohri	Page 80	Rosanne Cavalluzzi	Page 87	Ilene Tsui
Page 108	Shelly Verma	Page 122	Elizabeth Monahan		

VAN HOLTEN PRIMARY SCHOOL
Grade 2

Page 3	Kelly-Anne Stagi	Page 7	Kaitlin Miller	Page 8	Jimmy Bregartner
Page 13	Jessica Hansen	Page 15	Jamie Rosenstein	Page 30	David Guo
Page 43	Kelly Ford	Page 84	Michael Sutter	Page 98	Andrew Padavano
Page 112	Christina McGahan	Page 116	Jessica Yang	Page 121	Richa Pandey
Page 124	Philip McElroy				

From Millington, NJ
Page 114 David Testa, kindergarten

Contents

Chapter 3
Alligator Pie: Playing With Your Food.... 93

Eeny Meeny Miney Mine

A Chant for Picking the Best Library Book

by Ashley Maza and Judy Freeman, ©1992

Eeny meeny miney mine,

Catch a book by the spine;

If it hollers, let it whine,

Eeny meeny miney mine.

Miss Freeman says to pick

The very best book

And you are IT!

N THE LIBRARY ONE DAY, I WAS SCHMOOZING WITH A FOURTH-grade class as they were selecting books. "Which book is better?" one child asked, holding out one funny book and one scary mystery.

"Depends if you're in the mood for laughing or shivering," I said. "They're both terrific, but different. Take them both, maybe. Or 'eeny meeny' them. You know—eeny meeny miney mine . . ."

"Catch a book by the spine," chimed in classmate Ashley Maza.

"If it hollers, let it whine," I continued. "Eeny meeny miney mine."

Ashley finished up the newly constituted chant: "Miss Freeman says to pick the very best book and you are IT!"

Ever since, we use that chant to pick one book out of a batch.

Selecting three good library books out of a collection of thousands (at last count, there were 14,000 crammed into my little Van Holten School Library in Bridgewater, New Jersey) proves daunting to many children, and every gimmick helps. Whether it's a group of children plucking straws from your fist to win a coveted book for the week, or two kids flipping a Susan B. Anthony silver dollar to see who gets a book first, the object is to get many great books into the hands of children on a daily basis.

Love of language, which leads to the love of reading, starts at birth, with parents crooning nursery rhymes and singing the songs they heard from their parents. Songs, poems, and stories are all soulmates.

The purpose of *Hi Ho Librario!* is to demonstrate some of the ways songs and music can be used to get children excited about words, rhymes, stories, and books. Whether you are reading aloud to children, introducing a new unit in the curriculum, or presenting a mini-lesson, a related song, chant, or story can help children ease into a learning mood.

Ready to start a booktalk of new fiction titles? Having the group stand up and dance the Charleston to "Fiction, fiction; it's a made-up story from the author's brain" will get them relaxed and laughing, all the while reminding them of an easy-to-remember definition of the term "fiction." Singing Dennis Lee's "Alligator Pie" and composing new verses to the poem will help them discover that poetry is pleasurable to read and hear, and writing it is both challenging and fun. Singing the song "Ain't We Crazy?" with its abundance of homonyms, homophones, action verbs, paradoxes, and Lewis Carroll-like logic, will spice up that grammar lesson.

Singing crazy songs allows children an extra bit of freedom to act silly, to laugh, and to experiment with words and wordplay. Sometimes a song can help save the day. We had an unplanned fire drill that sent all 450 coatless kids and teachers streaming outside onto the blustery playground. After 20 frigid minutes, we were summoned to the gym to wait while the fire department investigated the alarm system. What does one do with all those squirming children in close quarters? The music teacher and I led everyone in a rousing rendition of "Throw It out the Window," the irreverent nursery rhyme song. When we were dismissed a few minutes later, the whole school was humming.

Often I'll hear a class in the hallway, and as the children pass the library, they will wave and start singing one of our songs, almost as a serenade. It gives me great satisfaction to know that the songs we sing now will be passed along and kept alive by new generations of singers. Look back into your childhood to recall the songs and musical situations that influenced you and share these stories with your children.

I have been singing and collecting songs as long as I can remember. One day, when I was six or seven, the family doctor made a house call (remember those days?) to check on me, home sick from school. There was a Weavers record on the record

player and I was in bed, singing along lustily, as Dr. Plotkin climbed to the top of the stairs. "She doesn't sound too sick to me," he commented, and I remember protesting indignantly that I was, too, sick—very sick, but that singing made me feel better.

Singing has always made me feel better.

As a child, I attended two wonderful Quaker summer camps: Camp Dark Waters in Medford, New Jersey, and Camp Echo Hill near Chestertown, Maryland. Singing was a natural and enjoyable part of each day, from singing competitions between tables at mealtimes to campfire songs at night. The songs I learned at camp I have never forgotten, and several of them are included in this collection.

Growing up in Havertown, Pennsylvania, I listened, with my ear suctioned against the wall of my bedroom, past my bedtime every Sunday night, to Gene Shay's folk music show on my brother Richard's radio in the next room. In fifth grade, I would sneak my sister Sharron's guitar whenever she wasn't home and figure out how the chords worked by reading her guitar book. In sixth grade, I begged for and received a ukulele, about which I gave an oral report and demonstration in Miss Froelich's class. In seventh grade, when my parents came home from vacation in Mexico lugging a huge guitar for my brother, I persuaded him to let me have it instead.

All three of us kids played guitar and sang folk songs, show tunes, and blues, while my mother walked around the house whistling and warbling big-band hits from the Forties with a mixture of the real words and her own, often off-the-wall lyrics. My father listened to classical music in the car and sang me songs like "Little Brown Jug,"

"There Is a Tavern in the Town," "Oh, My Name Is Samuel Hall," and "Smoke Gets in Your Eyes," which he said was a song that made him cry at age 16 when his first girlfriend dumped him for a rich boy. One of my earliest musical memories is of being crammed in the front seat of a car with Grampy, my mother's father, John Spiers, who was a "hoofer" in vaudeville, listening to him sing "Take Me Back to the Black Hills, the Black Hills of Dakota."

The high point of my elementary school years was in the fifth grade, when I sang "Doin' What Comes Natcherly" from the Broadway show *Annie Get Your Gun*, and the principal introduced me, saying, "And now, here's Judy Freeman, the little girl with the big voice." I still remember most of the words.

When I began working as a school librarian, I started collecting the songs of my youth and looking for new ones to pass along to my students. The rhymes of childhood have been around forever, and if you think back for a while you'll remember some of the ones you used to sing and chant. At school, giggling little girls take me aside in the library to belt out songs they just learned in Brownies. Friends like Louise Sherman, school librarian from Leonia, New Jersey, continue to feed me new songs heard at folk festivals and concerts. The market for singers who perform for children has mushroomed in the past ten years, led by artists like the affable Raffi and the innovative Tom Chapin.

Unfortunately, too many kids I meet have no access to this wealth of music for children. They listen to the radio and watch MTV, and if you ask them to sing you a favorite song, it's likely to be a pop song high on the charts. Aside from a once-a-week music period, many children never sing for pleasure.

When I started working as a librarian at Van Holten School, I discovered a nylon-stringed Yamaha guitar resting in the storage room and adopted it as my school guitar. The first time I brought it out to play, the dismayed reaction from my students was "You mean we hafta sing?"

Their disapproval didn't last long, and over the years many students have come back to the library to pay a visit from high school or college, saying, "I remember all the great songs you used to sing in here on the story rug. Where's The Beast?"

We named the guitar *The Beast* that first year; I can't remember why. We say his name slowly, with expression (the *Beast*), and every year, when I introduce him to kindergartners, they cringe when I tell them about him ("I'd like to introduce you to a particular friend of mine. Would you care to meet . . . the *Beast*? You would? Are you sure? You don't get scared easily . . . do you?"), and then they relax and giggle when they realize the ominous-sounding monster is really a guitar. My preschool classes of three- and four-year-old special-needs children love to strum his strings while I change chords for them, and many of my older kids have been inspired to take guitar lessons. I don't use the guitar for every class, and when I don't, someone always inquires, "Where's the *Beast*? Isn't he coming out today?"

This year I acquired a funny-looking little traveling guitar, a Martin Backpacker, that's all neck with no real body and weighs only two pounds. When I showed it to a class of first graders and told them I couldn't think of the perfect name,

Michael Nolan piped up, "I think you should call it *Bigfoot*." *Bigfoot* he is, and the children think of him as the *Beast*'s little brother.

Music is an intrinsic part of my library instructional program. Mnemonic devices performed as chants and songs help kids remember the parts of a book, the continents, the parts of speech. Songs are a natural and welcome help when introducing new stories or skills. Every year, when our students spend a grueling week taking their CATs (California Achievement Tests), I hold a CAT Test Sing in the library to help each class unwind. I print up a book of ten songs or so, with a copy for each student, and we spend the period singing silly nonsense songs. It's a reading activity as well, of course, and a poetry-writing activity—I have them compose new verses on the spot for at least one of the songs, which we then sing.

What better way to have children practice their reading than by handing out song lyrics to sing "with feeling," just as we want them to read aloud "with expression"? Somehow, even kids with reading difficulties can follow a songsheet after they've heard a song once or twice, as they start to memorize the words and see how they flow together.

Back in the olden days, the kindergarten teacher was expected to know how to play the piano well enough to accompany the children in daily singing. This is no longer an educational requirement for primary teachers, and with its demise has gone much of the day-to-day singing in the classroom, save for a daily a cappella version of "America" or "The Star-Spangled Banner."

"My kids get music once a week with the music teacher," some teachers argue. It's not enough. The so-called "specials"—art, music, physical education, library, computer lab—may be a welcome once-a-week time-out for students, but it is up to the classroom teacher to integrate them into the curriculum during the rest of the week. Creative teachers can always find a few extra minutes in an already-packed day to cover these "extras."

From my own observation, kids who sing together on a regular basis feel good about themselves and about their classmates. Not enough schools have weekly assemblies where everyone sings a few songs together before or after the performance.

"I can't sing," teachers and librarians protest at my workshops when I whip out a guitar to do a song that ties in just right with a new book. It's not true, of course. Most of us can sing just fine. You don't have to sound like Streisand or Sinatra to sing with children, because children don't care how we sound. Enthusiasm counts for everything; staying in tune is a bonus, but not actually necessary.

In my first job at Clinton School in Plainfield, New Jersey, there was an extraordinary preschool teacher named Marge Cohen who sang with her class all the time. Marge's voice was down in the basement—a low bass—while the kids' voices were up in the attic—high-pitched peeps. It never made the slightest difference. The class would belt out songs with abandon, and no one cared a whit that they were singing in a variety of keys. It's the enthusiasm, the love of songs, and the feeling of warmth and being connected with others that's important.

Teachers who still insist they can't sing can always use songs as chants or poetry, or—as my friend, children's book author Penny Pollock, reminds me—they can always form an impromptu rhythm band to recite the songs while banging out the tempo on triangles, spoons, cymbals, pencils, bells, or anything else handy that makes a nice noise. Simply clapping hands and tapping feet is enough to make kids and teachers feel musical together.

Over the years I've collected, written, and set to music hundreds of songs, poems, stories, and chants. For this collection I've concentrated on three general subject areas that give me great pleasure: books and reading, nonsense and folklore, and food. Included for each selection are words, music, and guitar chords; background information and ideas for using that song with books or in your day-to-day teaching; plus an annotated bibliography of children's book tie-ins, all of them top-notch read-alouds you can use to present the song and vice versa.

I keep a list of all my songs handy, and when planning to showcase a new book, I skim the list to see if I can pull in a song to warm up or wrap up the reading session. In the annotated booklist that follows each song in this book, I have tried to gather together an eclectic array of children's books with similar themes or motifs or moods that complement the song or extend its range.

Just as many of us can remember where we were when we first heard an oldie now playing on the radio, children can connect a song they know to a book on the same theme. Reading Mary Jane Auch's *Eggs Mark the Spot,* about a hen who lays artistic eggs, will get them humming, "Oh, I had a little chicken and she wouldn't lay an egg," and they'll never forget it if you pull out a hard-boiled egg and crack it open as a finale.

Present the concept of exaggeration and the form of the tall tale by first singing "The Biggest Book." Children can pick out the phrases in each verse that stretch the truth. Then continue with a tall-tale masterpiece such as *Swamp Angel* by Anne Isaacs and examine the tall-tale elements within. The bibliography following "The Biggest Book" consists of other tall tales (Sid Fleischman's *McBroom Tells the Truth*, James Stevenson's *Brrr!*); cautionary tales that show the importance of books and reading (David Day's *The Sleeper*, Patricia Polacco's *Aunt Chip and the Great Triple Creek Dam Affair*, and Mark Teague's *Frog Medicine*); humorous stories about books (Henrik Drescher's *Simon's Book*, John F. Green's *Alice and the Birthday Giant*, and Jon Scieszka's *The Stinky Cheese Man and Other Fairly Stupid Tales*), and two thought-provoking folktales, each about a peddler who heeds a dream that brings him good fortune connected with reading (Gail E. Haley's *Dream Peddler* and Margaret Hodges's *Saint Patrick and the Peddler*). My hope is that each brief booklist will start you thinking of other equally effective titles and activities to go along with the song.

When you introduce a new song to your kids, it's nice but not always necessary to give them the written words. It depends on the song and the emphasis you are placing on it, but many kids love having the words on paper and save each handout. Sing the song at least twice, and then, the following day or week, do it yet again so kids can learn it by heart.

Ask students to write new verses, make up hand motions or dance steps, or act out a song, and tape record them singing, so they can hear themselves. Songs can be used

to reinforce a variety of comprehension skills. After listening to the song "Henry, My Son" and joining in on the refrain, "Mother, be quick, I've got to be sick and lay me down to die," second graders will be able to sing the whole song the second time, as they recall the sequence of each verse, retelling the amusing story of an unfortunate young man who went into the woods and ate snakes. And third through sixth graders, exhorted to listen closely for clues in "Who Threw the Overalls in Mrs. Murphy's Chowder?" will be able to infer and explain just how those overalls came to be in the pot.

I've tried to give germs of ideas for using each song as a tie-in to daily classroom and library life, and I hope each small suggestion will strike a chord with you and resonate as you design lessons to keep kids humming.

Pull out a prop to go with a song: a teacup for "I Sat Next to the Duchess at Tea" or a box of doughnut holes for "I Went to Cincinnati" ("Oh I Had a Little Chicken"). Sometimes, an off-the-cuff idea will snowball. Looking at the story "Cecil Was a Caterpillar," where the insect devours all the cabbages in his town, county, state, country, hemisphere, and world, you might say, "Hmm. I was just planning to start a letter-writing unit. I could introduce the concept of addresses and have each child write a letter to Cecil, setting up the envelope correctly with his or her home address and Cecil's full address. We could make coleslaw for a snack and do a measurement lesson for math. For our science unit on animals, I've always wanted to hatch a monarch butterfly. Better get some butterfly books from the library. Then, for reading, we could read some of the swallowing stories listed in the bibliography for "Hoimie the Woim." Before you know it, you've planned your week's lessons, all thanks to one hungry caterpillar.

Another popular follow-up to singing is to distribute copies of the song and see how children interpret it in pictures. Many of the illustrations in this book were done by students in grades two and three at Van Holten School. Thanks to teachers Loretta Ark, Marin Eisenstat, LouAnn Parrino, Barbara Storen, Cindy Williams, Kurt Weaver, Laura Coughlin, Matt Barbosa, and Julie Kotcho, and to art teacher Dolores Rowland, who worked with many of the classes to discuss technique and style and got the kids fired up. Linda Forte's and Sandy Vitale's fourth-grade classes at Eisenhower School and Carol Shields's and Evelyn Balunis's fifth-grade classes at Hillside School also contributed their artwork. Each class learned three of the songs in the book, and children contributed hundreds of marvelous drawings, as they experienced firsthand what it means when we sing, "The illustrator draws."

I'd love to hear from teachers, librarians, and parents who have undertaken new projects with the selections in this book. May the following songs and suggestions help you to loosen up your children and get them excited about words, language, books, reading, singing, and trading marvelous nonsense with each other.

Chapter 1

Hi Ho Librario!

Songs and Chants
About Books and Reading

THIS FIRST SECTION OF THE BOOK AND ACCOMPANYING recording focus on songs that lead children to books and familiarize them with books and libraries. As an elementary school librarian, I find it's important to be chauvinistic when defending my domain. Too many school districts have under-funded or defunded their library programs, which is a travesty if we are serious about getting children excited about reading and writing. Teachers can't possibly keep abreast of the vast range of materials available to them with 5,000 new children's books being published each year. No one can keep up with that proliferation, but a good librarian distills the best of it and makes it instantly available and accessible to teachers and children.

"The library should feel like home," I tell my students at the beginning of the year when I go over what I expect of them. "Not your bedroom—it's too messy, with all those dirty socks and things. Not the living room—it's too neat and formal." (When I said that, one of my students announced that her mother didn't allow her to go into the living room. "She knows if I go in there, too, because she can see my footprints on the carpet." Whew. May our libraries never be that forbidding!) "The library should feel as cozy, comfortable, and welcoming as your family room on a good day, after the newspapers and toys have been cleaned up some."

I teach 20 classes a week in my library, ranging now from preschool to third grade, and my aim is to have them know the library inside out by the time they move on to the upper elementary school. To that end, we read, tell, booktalk, write about, illustrate, and act out books and stories; recite poems and sing songs; tell dumb jokes; play games that reinforce book and library vocabulary; explore fiction, nonfiction, biography, and reference; and celebrate all genres and styles of literature.

I know we are doing something right and useful and important when I hear teachers tell me, "My kids can't wait to come to the library."

"I love the library," kids say every day. "It's one of my favorite places."

"Mine, too," I tell them.

In the library, I reinforce classroom teaching about caring for and valuing books with the help of the following songs, which stress the importance and pleasures of reading, of digging out all the best books lurking on the shelves, and of letting books speak to us.

Hi Ho Librario!

Grade Level: K–3

The author writes the book, the author writes the book;
Hi Ho Librario, the author writes the book.

The illustrator draws, the illustrator draws;
Hi Ho Librario, the illustrator draws.

The publisher puts it together, the publisher puts it together;
Hi Ho Librario, the publisher puts it together.

The copyright tells us when they made the book, and then,
Hi Ho Librario, let's sing it once again.

ONE DAY MY GOOD FRIEND AND FELLOW LIBRARIAN JANE Scherer called. "I just wrote a library song," she told me, all pleased, and she sang "Hi Ho Librario" for me over the phone. I have written several book-related songs to help my students remember the parts of books and catalog cards, and I consider hers a classic. It is a natural for getting kids to remember the key terms *author*, *illustrator*, *publisher*, and *copyright* as you sing the song over and over.

Some children can sing a song a dozen times without getting bored, while others begin to whine if you sing a song twice. "Again?" they'll moan. "Not again!" So I turn this song into a game that we *can* sing over and over while the meaning and vocabulary really sink in.

First we review the parts of the title page of the picture book I have just read aloud to them and locate the book's "birthday," or copyright date. As I start singing the song, children chime right in, picking up the words as we go. The first time, they tend to sing, "Hi ho the derry-o," until I correct them. "We're singing about a library. So naturally, it's got to be 'Hi Ho LIBRARIO!'"

Now we start over, singing it *very* slowly. At the end of the last verse, I chant, "Oh no! We've got to sing it again. A little bit faster, a little bit better," and we speed it up a bit the second time through. This acknowledges the impatient kids and gets them tuned in to the humor of the situation.

By the fifth time, we're singing it at breakneck speed, and I yell, "Someone say 'STOP!'" Someone always does. "Thanks," I tell the now-giggling class. "I thought we were going to have to keep singing it until we exploded."

Hi Ho Librario!

Words by Jane Scherer, ©1982; to the tune of "The Farmer in the Dell"

The au - thor writes the book, the

au - thor writes the book; Hi Ho Li -

brar - i - o, the au - thor writes the book.

Children's Books to Use with "Hi Ho Librario!"

Bonsall, Crosby. *Tell Me Some More.* Illus. by Fritz Siebel. Harper & Row, 1961. (ISBN 0-06-020601-2; unp.; Grades PreK–1)

In a classic from the I Can Read series, Andrew regales his skeptical friend Tim with stories of a special place where he can pat a lion, be taller than a tree, or pick up a river and never get wet, and he takes him there—to the library, where books are filled with every wonder.

Caseley, Judith. *Sophie and Sammy's Library Sleepover.* Illus. by the author. Greenwillow, 1993. (ISBN 0-688-10616-1; unp.; Grades PreK–1)

Sophie adores the nighttime library story-time with librarian Mrs. Terry and feels guilty about her little brother Sammy staying home, until she plans a special bedroom story program just for him.

Duvoisin, Roger. *Petunia.* Illus. by the author. Knopf, 1950. (ISBN 0-394-82589-6; unp.; Grades K–2)

Finding a book in her meadow and deciding to carry it around with her, silly goose Petunia fancies herself wise and begins to give foolish advice to the other barnyard animals, who believe she can read.

Freeman, Don. *Quiet! There's a Canary in the Library.* Illus. by the author. Children's Press, 1969. (ISBN 0-516-08737-1; unp.; Grades PreK–1)

On a Saturday morning at the library, Carey imagines herself the librarian, welcoming and assisting all the wild animals, who cause a rumpus.

Hutchins, Pat. *The Tale of Thomas Mead.* Illus. by the author. Greenwillow, 1980. (ISBN 0-688-84282-8; unp.; Grades K–2)

In a bouncy rhyming saga, a stubborn young boy refuses to learn how to read, replying, "Why should I?" to the exasperated folks he meets, until he's jailed for jaywalking and as a prisoner finally is induced to crack a book.

McGovern, Ann. *Drop Everything, It's D.E.A.R. Time!* Illus. by Anna DiVito. Scholastic, 1993. (ISBN 0-590-45802-7; unp.; Grades K–2)

It's just a normal, busy day at school until "Drop Everything and Read" time, when all stop what they are doing and settle down with a good book. If your school has no D.E.A.R. time scheduled, this story may help convince the administration that it's time to start.

McPhail, David. *Fix-It.* Illus. by the author. Dutton, 1984. (ISBN 0-525-44093-3; unp.; Grades PreK–1)

Though little bear Emma's parents and the fix-it man all try to fix the TV, it won't work. A distraught Emma finds no solace until her mother reads her a book.

McPhail, David. *Lost!* Illus. by the author. Joy Street/Little, Brown, 1990. (ISBN 0-316-56329-3; unp.; Grades PreK–1)

When a city boy and his new friend, a lost bear, can't figure out the way home, they try the library for better directions.

McPhail, David. *Santa's Book of Names.* Illus. by the author. Little, Brown, 1993. (ISBN 0-316-56335-8; unp.; Grades K–2)

Helping Santa deliver gifts when the old guy loses his specs, nonreader Edward has no choice but to decipher Santa's written gift list.

Mennen, Ingrid, and Niki Daly. *Somewhere in Africa.* Illus. by Nicolaas Maritz. Dutton, 1992. (ISBN 0-525-44848-9; unp.; Grades K–2)

South African city boy Ashraf loves reading about wild African animals from his favorite book, which he renews at the library over and over.

Book Chants

By Judy Freeman, ©1995
Grade Level: 1–6

We do book chants at the beginning of a lesson or anytime I want to check whether the children remember what and where each type of book is. The chants are simplifications of the definitions of each type, but they allow you to gauge instantly what kids remember.

Fiction Chant

• • • •
Fiction, fiction,

• • • • • • •
It's a made-up story from the author's brain.

(MOTIONS: Bend your arms at the elbows, hands and forearms raised, and rotate/wave both arms from left to right, "windshield-wiper style," in time to the chant. The dots above the words indicate a "wipe" in the opposite direction.)

After we do this chant seated, I tell the kids about the fabulous dance craze of the 1920s, the Charleston, that their great-grandparents probably did. We then stand up and do the chant's first line with a Charleston kick and the second with bent knees, crisscrossing our hands quickly back and forth.

Nonfiction Chant

• • • • • • •
Numbers mean nonfiction, numbers mean nonfiction;
• • • • • • •
Yes they do, yes they're true, numbers mean nonfiction.

(MOTIONS: Wag your outstretched index fingers in time to the chant. The dots above the words indicate each wag.)

(criss   cross   roll hands   clap)
Nonfiction books have facts, that's true;

(criss   cross   roll hands   clap)
Nonfiction books have facts, that's true.

(MOTIONS: For each line, criss-cross arms twice, once right over left and once left over right, roll hands around each other, and clap on the word "true." Or have your students make up new motions. Who says you can't have aerobics in the library or classroom?)

I WISH I COULD REMEMBER THE IDENTITY OF THE LIBRARIAN who taught me the first line of this chant. It is such a useful one for children, who often can't help thinking that nonfiction means not true. The librarian took one of my professional development courses on children's literature at Rutgers University some years back. I always use part of one session to make a tape with the class of songs, chants, poems, riddles, and other kid-based trivia. Everyone contributes to the taping, and everyone gets a copy of the tape to use with his or her students. It's a great way to compile a lot of good, useful storytelling material in a short time. This also works well with a class of children, with each person responsible for reciting a song or chant learned at home or from a book.

I added the second line of the chant, and I do it with the kids as an obnoxious, in-your-face whine. This is in direct response to my brother Richard and sister Sharron, who tortured me, at the tender age of three, with their pointed fingers wagging in my face, chanting in singsong voices, "I'm gonna put Judy in the baby carriage, I'm gonna put Judy in the baby carriage." I'd cry and scream at the indignity of their suggesting that I, a baby no longer, should consent to be relegated back to the baby carriage.

When I teach this chant to my first and second graders, I relate that dire childhood memory. Children love to hear stories about when their teachers were children, especially the embarrassing parts.

In terms of the information included in the chants, when I ask students if a book is fiction or nonfiction or I want them to tell me the difference, all I need to do to stimulate their memories is point my index fingers at them and sing, "Nah nah nah nah nah nah," and they remember.

At the same time as you generalize with your students that fiction books are made-up stories and nonfiction books are true, don't forget to add a "BUT!" Not all nonfiction books are true, with fairy tales, jokes and riddles, and poetry being the most obvious exceptions, and many fiction books are based on true events. Life is full of exceptions, and libraries are too.

Renee Jackson, friend and fellow librarian, in trying to figure out both an effortless mnemonic device and a way to stress the broader definition of nonfiction, came up with a wonderful new chant to the tune of "Miss Mary Mack."

First through third graders love singing this, and many will memorize it on the spot. Present it as a kickoff to a unit on locating and using nonfiction.

For a first lesson, after singing the ditty, introduce a broad spectrum of nonfiction books, including those exceptions that are not typically true: poetry, plays, folklore, and riddles. To run through the ten categories of Dewey, preselect a pile of interesting books, one from each hundred, that illustrate the general subject. Hold up and show a bit of each book, define its subject, and then mention other compelling subjects within the category. In the 500s, for instance, show an experiment book from the 507.8s and then point out astronomy (520s), earthquakes and volcanoes (551.2), tornadoes (551.5), rocks (552), dinosaurs (567.9), plants (580s), and animals (590s).

Ode to Nonfiction

I am a non- non- non- nonfiction
Book book book,
With lots of facts facts facts,
Just take a look look look.

There's information, oh yes,
And things to do do do,
Open me up up up,
And I'll help you you you.

Most times I'm true true true,
Sometimes I'm not not not,
Plays, poems, jokes jokes jokes,
Folktales I've got got got.

Just check my number number number,
Upon my spine spine spine,
Subjects together gether gether,
All in a line line line.

Ode to Nonfiction

Words by Renee Jackson, ©1996; to the tune of "Miss Mary Mack"

I am a non - non - non - non - fic - tion

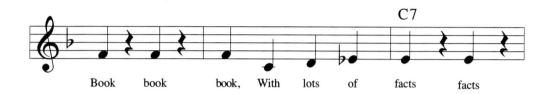

Book book book, With lots of facts facts

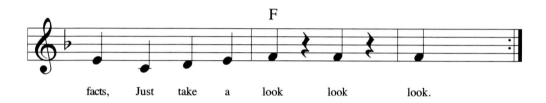

facts, Just take a look look look.

Biography Chant

(Snap fingers after each syllable of bi-[SNAP] o-[SNAP] gra-[SNAP] phy [SNAP])

  • • • •   • •

Bi-o-gra-phy; they're in alphabetical order *(CLAP, CLAP)*

(hands on hips)   *(point both index fingers at someone)*

By the *famous* person's last name — *not the author*;

             • •

They're in alphabetical order *(CLAP, CLAP)*

(hands on hips)   *(point both index fingers at someone)*

By the *famous* person's last name — *not the author*!

(MOTIONS: The dots above the words indicate each time you snap your fingers, elbows bent, arms swinging back on each snap.)

CHILDREN ENJOY TAKING APART WORDS AND TINKERING WITH them. When talking to children about biographies, write the word "biography" on the board and then show them how to dissect it. "Bio" comes from the Greek "bios," which means life, and "graphy" comes from the Greek "graphon" or "graphos," which means to write.

Inform your listeners that an autobiography is *not* the written life story of a car. "Auto" is Greek for self, so an autobiography is a self-life-written story.

When I was student-teaching at Irving School in Highland Park, New Jersey, in 1973, I spent time working with librarian Sally Edmondson, who covered three schools and was always glad for an extra pair of hands. I was planning to get my MLS from Rutgers and was eager to log a little experience. I mended, carded, and shelved books and filed new cards in the catalog. One day I took a good look at a section of the nonfiction shelves that was unfamiliar to me: the biographies. "Look at this," I remember thinking. "These shelves are a mess. I'll be a helpful person and fix them up."

They didn't appear to be in any particular order, so I started rearranging them alphabetically by the author's last name. As I was finishing my task, Mrs. Edmondson came out to see what I was doing. "Look," I told her. "All these books were out of order, so I redid them for you."

She looked and gave a little scream. "These are biographies," she said. "Don't you know that biographies are in alphabetical order by the *famous* person's last name — *not the author?*"

I didn't then, but I sure do now. When I explain the embarrassing background of the chant to my students, I tell them I can still feel my cheeks blushing whenever I say the words "*not the author!*"

SEE BOOK-RELATED TITLES LISTED UNDER "THE BOOK SONG," PAGE 24.

The Book Song

Grade Level: 2–5

The name of the book is the title,
The person who wrote it's the author,
The illustrator drew the pictures,
The publisher put it together,
The copyright tells us when it was published.

The back of the book is the spine,
The paper cover is the dust jacket;
On the spine you'll find a label,
A small white paper label,
With the call number or the call letters.

Call numbers mean books of nonfiction,
Arranged in numerical order.
When it's true, it's nonfiction,
All loaded with facts
And information about all subjects.

If it's fiction, it's a made-up story
That comes from the brain of the author;
Both E, which stands for easy,
And FIC, which stands for fiction,
Are in ABC order by the author's last name.

This is a song about books,
And how they're arranged in the library;
We hope you won't forget it,
And you'll learn it with care,
So you'll know where everything is located.
We hope you won't forget it,
And you'll learn it with care,
So you'll know where everything is located.

EVER NOTICE HOW MUCH EASIER IT IS TO REMEMBER WHAT you sing than what you read? Many years back, trying to find interesting new ways for my students to retain book-related vocabulary, I started singing to myself what it was I wanted them to remember. Before long, I had written a solemn-sounding tune for my second graders.

To introduce the song, I hand out the printed text of the words to each child. I sing the first verse and then repeat it so they can try it along with me, and then we sing the whole song together with flourish and just a touch of pomposity and mock serious-ness.

The following week, the children sing the song once again, still using the printed words, and then I ask them to turn the paper over so we can "sing in the blanks." I tell them it's like filling in the blanks, only with singing instead of talking. (Teachers, of course, will recognize it as a variation on the cloze technique.) "Sing as much of the song as you remember. You will be amazed that, even though you've only sung this song twice before, you will be able to remember most of the words. Your brain is so quick and so sharp, it has practically memorized the entire song." They sit there eying me skeptically, but sure enough, when we start to sing they find they know at least the key words, and many can sing it straight through.

I sing "The name of a book is the . . . ," and they sing, "Title," and we keep going. In this way it is possible to reinforce effortlessly many book concepts, includ-ing the arrangement of the library into fiction and nonfiction areas.

The Book Song

Words and music by Judy Freeman, ©1995

The name of the book is the ti_____ tle, the per - son who wrote it's the au_____ thor,_____ the il - lu - stra - tor drew the pic - tures, the pub - li - sher put it to - ge - ther; the co - py - right tells us when it was pub - lished._____

We hope you won't for - get it,———— and you'll learn it with care, so you'll know where ev - 'ry - thing is lo———— ca - ted.————

Children's Books to Use with "The Book Song"

Christelow, Eileen. *What Do Authors Do?* Illus. by the author. Clarion, 1995. (ISBN 0-395-71124-X; unp.; Grades 1–4)

When two neighbors, both of them writers, watch Rufus the dog chase Max the cat, we see how two people can use the same idea and write completely different types of stories. We follow their progress through revisions, editing, and publishing.

Cummings, Pat, comp. and ed. *Talking with Artists.* Bradbury, 1992. (ISBN 0-02-724245-5; 96p.; Grades 2–6)

Meet 14 well-known children's book illustrators who describe where they get their ideas, how they got started as artists, and how they work.

Cummings, Pat, ed. *Talking with Artists, Volume 2.* Simon & Schuster, 1995. (ISBN 0-689-80310-9; 96p.; Grades 2–6)

Here are fascinating conversations, color photos, and sample artworks from 13 more children's book illustrators, including Kevin Henkes, Brian Pinkney, and Vera B. Williams.

Daugherty, James. *Andy and the Lion.* Illus. by the author. Viking, 1938. (ISBN 0-670-12433-8; unp.; Grades K–2)

Andy is still thinking about the lions in his library book when he encounters a real lion with a thorn stuck in its paw and, like Androcles in the old Greek tale, he removes it.

Falwell, Cathryn. *The Letter Jesters.* Illus. by the author. Ticknor & Fields, 1994. (ISBN 0-395-66898-0; unp.; Grades 2–4)

In this jazzy picture book, two jesters, accompanied by their perky dog Typo, present many sizes and styles of typefaces and demonstrate how typography can evoke various responses in readers.

Huff, Barbara A. *Once Inside the Library.* Illus. by Iris Van Rynback. Little, Brown, 1990. (ISBN 0-316-37967-0; unp.; Grades 1–3)

Discover through this illustrated poem all the places you can go in your imagination and marvels you can uncover with the books in your library. Try this as a choral reading with your kids.

King-Smith, Dick. *The School Mouse*. Illus. by Cynthia Fisher. Hyperion, 1995. (ISBN 0-7868-2029-2; 124p.; Grades 1–5)

From her hiding place above the kindergarten teacher's desk, mouse Flora watches the children and learns to read, a vital skill that saves her life. You'll appreciate her mouse alphabet rhyme: "A B C D E F G / Oh, what clever mice are we! / H I J K L M N / Mice are just as bright as men. / O P Q R S T U / And to prove that this is true, / V and W X Y Z / That's the alphabet, you see!"

Knowlton, Jack. *Books and Libraries*. Illus. by Harriet Barton. HarperCollins, 1991. (ISBN 0-06-021610-7; 36p.; Grades 2–5)

Starting with cave writing in southern France thirty thousand years ago, here is a history of books and writing, explaining how picture writing and hieroglyphics give way to the Greek alphabet, Roman libraries, Gutenberg's movable type, U.S. libraries, and Melvil Dewey's decimal system.

Krensky, Steven. *Breaking into Print: Before and After the Invention of the Printing Press*. Illus. by Bonnie Christensen. Little, Brown, 1996. (ISBN 0-316-50376-2; 32p.; Grades 2–5)

The invention of the printing press revolutionized bookmaking, which Krensky traces from medieval monks' handwriting on parchment to Gutenberg's Bibles, published in 1456.

Marshall, James. *Wings: A Tale of Two Chickens*. Illus. by the author. Viking, 1986. (ISBN 0-670-80961-6; unp.; Grades K–2)

Bored chicken Winnie, who hasn't a lick of sense because she never reads, is taken in by a smooth-talking fox when he invites her aboard his hot-air balloon. After reading, your class can come up with a list: Ten Ways Books and Reading Can Save Your Life.

Nixon, Joan Lowery. *If You Were a Writer*. Illus. by Bruce Degen. Four Winds, 1988. (ISBN 0-02-768210-2; unp.; Grades 1–3)

Melia's mother, a writer, tells her what writers do, from working with words and searching for ideas to inventing characters and helping a story idea grow.

Rumford, James. *The Cloudmakers*. Illus. by the author. Houghton Mifflin, 1996. (ISBN 0-395-76505-6; unp.; Grades 1–4)

Captured by Arab warriors, an old Chinese man and his grandson bargain for their release by promising to make special clouds for the Great Sultan, who is delighted when the "clouds" turn out to be handmade paper. This one's a great lead-in to a paper-making project.

Stevens, Janet. *From Pictures to Words: A Book About Making a Book*. Illus. by the author. Holiday House, 1995. (ISBN 0-8234-1154-0; unp.; Grades 1–4)

Stevens describes how she came to write, illustrate, and publish her first story with the help of her main characters: Koala Bear, Cat, and Rhino.

Swallow, Pam. *Melvil and Dewey in the Chips*. Illus. by Judith Brown. Shoe Tree, 1986. (ISBN 0-936915-03-X; 47p.; Grades 1–4)

Ripe for adventure and excitement, school library gerbil Dewey fast-talks his reluctant friend and cagemate Melvil to bust out of the cage and explore the library and the school.

Williams, Barbara. *The Author and Squinty Gritt*. Illus. by Betsy James. Dutton, 1990. (ISBN 0-525-44655-9; 67p.; Grades 1–3)

Famous children's book author Helena Wright is visiting Squinty's school, and the second grader decides to enter the school contest for best poster to win the author's special prize, which he figures could be a drive to her mansion in her red sports car.

The Card Catalog Song

Grade Level: 2–5

CHORUS:
> In the catalog, in the catalog,
> in the card card catalog;
> Just take a look, you can find any book
> in the card card catalog.

The author card has the author on top,
Last name first, comma, first name after that;
You'll notice one card for each book written by
That author if you really try.
CHORUS

The title card has the title on top,
Title underneath, author in the middle;
It's a certain kind of sandwich we
Titled the bologna.
CHORUS

The subject card has the subject on top,
In capital letters; it's so different from the title,
Cause it tells you what that book's about;
So find the book and sign it out.
CHORUS

When you want the address of a book,
Look up the author or the subject or the title;
Find the call number on the upper left side;
The card catalog is your guide.
CHORUS

The Card Catalog Song

Words and music by Judy Freeman, ©1984

In the ca — ta - log, — in the

ca — ta - log, — in the card card ca - ta - log; — Just

take a — look, you can find an - y book in the

card card ca — ta - log. —

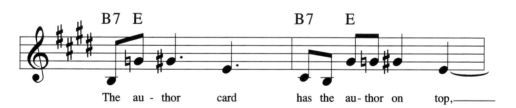

The au - thor card has the au - thor on top, —

last name first, com - ma, first name af - ter that, You'll

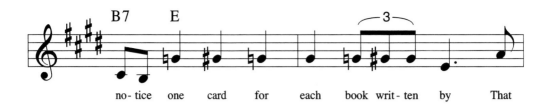

no- tice   one   card   for   each   book   writ- ten   by   That

auth - or   if   you   real——   ly   try.

N MY HALF-HOUR DRIVE TO WORK EACH DAY, I OFTEN SING ALONG with the radio, learn to tell new stories I've taped myself reading, and muse about my upcoming day's classes. One day I started thinking about the card catalog and how too many of my students had trouble distinguishing between the author, title, and subject cards. By the time I got to work, the chorus was humming through my head, and I raced into school to write down the words before they escaped. The rest of it I wrote on a train ride to Philadelphia. I think of it as my transportation song.

If you're scratching your head over my reference to a "bologna sandwich" in the second verse, it's really quite simple. As I demonstrate with oversized catalog cards or on the white board, I tell kids, "Picture, if you will, a lovely bologna sandwich. There's a nice slice of bread on the bottom"—I point to the title under the author's name—"and an identical slice of bread on top"—I point to the title on the top line of the card.

"Let's try making a bologna sandwich." We pantomime placing a slice of bread on our palms. Next the slice of bologna. On top, the other slice of bread.

"Now, look closely at the bologna. What do you observe?"

Someone always calls out, "It's sticking out over the side of the bread."

"Exactly! Now take a look at this catalog card. Notice the author's name sticking out on the left side? That's our bologna. Everyone knows authors are full of beans and full of bologna. That's how they can write so many fabulous books."

Works for me.

```
                    Hi ho librario!
784.6       Freeman, Judy.
F                   Hi ho librario! / Bala Cynwyd, PA: Rock Hill Press,
            ©1997.
                    144p. illus.


            1. Songs. I. Title.


A BOLOGNA SANDWICH          ●
```

Singing the card catalog song with second and third graders works well. I hand out a copy of the words to each child and tell them it's a very tongue-twisty song that reveals almost everything one needs to know about "the brains of the library." We call our card catalog "The Major Brain." Afterward, we explore the catalog, looking up strange or familiar subjects, authors, and titles, then finding books on the shelves. Letting our fingers do the walking, we have fun in the catalog. At various times children look for books published the year they were born, check to see if they can find their names or names of family members in there, look up books they already know and love, search out the oldest books in the library, find one fiction and one nonfiction book on the same subject, and, at the end of each discovery session, show-and-tell their results to the rest of the class.

And then we computerized our library. Many libraries deep-six their card catalogs once they've computerized. I haven't had the heart to do so yet, but it's coming in the next year or so. Our students are still tested on yearly standardized tests about their knowledge of information found on a catalog card. Also, I find it's easier to teach classes about the card catalog first so everyone can have simultaneous hands-on practice, and then we move on to how the computer catalog works. Also, I really like the card catalog. It's such an endearing and friendly piece of furniture, and in it, as author Penny Pollock says, "You find the best stuff by accident."

We call the new computers "Einstein," named by first grader Phillip McElroy because, as he said, "Einstein knew everything about the world, and the computer knows everything about what's in our library."

Once the catalog is gone, I'll miss all our hands-on sessions, though we'll continue to use our miniature catalog (really a 30-drawer tool kit) filled with miniature subjects (several hundred objects ranging from tiny animals to a one-inch bright blue bathtub) and 1-by-2-inch cards, each with the name of an author or title, sorted alphabetically, through which we learn alphabetizing, categorizing, and information retrieval skills.

On the other hand, I'm thrilled that the library is finally fully automated. I can check in materials in a fraction of the time, and it makes my scores of daily searches for materials for kids and teachers a cinch. In keeping with these changes, I recently updated the lyrics to the "Card Catalog Song" as follows:

In the Automated Catalog

Words and music by Judy Freeman, ©1996
Grade Level: 2–5

CHORUS:
> In the catalog, in the catalog,
>
> in the automated catalog;
>
> Just take a look, you can find any book
>
> in the automated catalog.

The catalog will help you search,

Type in the author, subject, keyword, or the title;

It will tell you if the book's on the shelf,

So you can check it out yourself.

CHORUS

The author's name's juggled on the screen,

Last name first, comma, first name after that;

You'll see an entry for each book written by

That author if you really try.

CHORUS

The keyword search is the best of the bunch

When you're not sure of the title and you just forgot the author;

Type in one keyword and if you persist,

The computer generates a list.

CHORUS

Looking for the address of a book,

See the illustrator, pub. and date, the pagination, annotation;

All the info you retrieve,

The computer has up its sleeve.

CHORUS

Children's Books to Use with "The Card Catalog Song"

Bradby, Marie. *More Than Anything Else.* Illus. by Chris K. Soentpiet. Orchard, 1995. (ISBN 0-531-08764-6; 32p.; Grades 1–6)

In a fictionalized episode from the life of African American educator Booker T. Washington, we meet him in post-Civil War West Virginia as a nine-year-old boy who burns with the desire to learn to read.

Bunting, Eve. *The Wednesday Surprise.* Illus. by Donald Carrick. Clarion, 1989. (ISBN 0-89919-721-3; unp.; Grades K–4)

Grandma and Anna are planning an important surprise for Dad's birthday: Anna has taught Grandma how to read.

Duffey, Betsy. *Utterly Yours, Booker Jones.* Viking, 1995. (ISBN 0-670-86007-7; 116p.; Grades 4–6)

When asked to write a speech to save his school mascot, usually prolific seventh grader Booker experiences his first writer's block.

Heide, Florence Parry, and Judith Heide Gilliland. *The Day of Ahmed's Secret.* Illus. by Ted Lewin. Lothrop, 1990. (ISBN 0-688-08895-3; unp.; Grades 1–4)

After a young Egyptian boy makes his daily rounds through contemporary Cairo, selling cooking-gas canisters to earn money for his family, he reveals his proud secret: He has just learned to write his name.

Hopkins, Lee Bennett, sel. *Good Books, Good Times!* Illus. by Harvey Stevenson. Harper & Row, 1990. (ISBN 0-06-022528-9; 32p.; Grades K–4)

Celebrate the triumphs and fun of reading with 14 delectable poems that make a definitive case for books.

Lindbergh, Anne. *Travel Far, Pay No Fare.* HarperCollins, 1992. (ISBN 0-06-021775-8; 199p.; Grades 5–7)

As Owen's children's-book-writing mother and Parsley's father prepare for their upcoming wedding, Owen discovers how Parsley, using her new bookmark, has somehow entered into her favorite books to catnap the cats from each one and bring them home with her.

Sobol, Donald J. *Encyclopedia Brown, Boy Detective.* Illus. by Leonard Shortall. Nelson, 1963. (ISBN 0-525-67200-1; 83p.; Grades 3–6)

Use this first book in the long-running popular series to introduce America's young Sherlock-Holmes-in-sneakers as he employs his encyclopedic memory to solve ten cases.

Alas and Alack: The Wounded Book's Lament

Grade Level: 2–6

As I was a-walking the hallways of my school,
I spied the library, the door open wide;
I stopped in to browse, take a look at some fiction,
When one of the volumes cried out from inside.

CHORUS:
      Alas, alack, please don't hurt me or bruise me,
      Don't crayon my pages or damage my spine;
      Don't lead me to water for I'll not enjoy it,
      Don't spill your food on me when you stop to dine.

The last child who read me thought not of my feelings,
He turned down my pages, his bookmark was gone;
His dog came and sniffed me, he chewed up my binding,
He left me thus wounded outside on the lawn.
CHORUS

Now I am not one who would treat a book badly;
I am a kind person, I'd not hurt a flea;
But hearing these cries and the sad lamentations,
I stopped to consider the book's words to me.
CHORUS

"I swear I'll be different," I promised that volume,
"I know you can trust me to treat you with care.
For I've been a reader for many fine years now,
Turned thousands of pages with never a tear."

FINAL CHORUS:

"Then please teach the others," the book did beseech me,

"For I am afraid of their coarse, hurtful ways."

"I'll do that," I promised, for books are our treasures,

"I'll champion your cause for the rest of my days."

I HAVE ALWAYS LOVED COWBOY SONGS, FINDING THEM SO HEART-breakingly tragic and tough at the same time. So when I set out to write a song about treating library books with kindness, love, and respect, I found myself thinking about poor dying cowboys in songs like "The Streets of Laredo," "When the Work's All Done This Fall," and "Bury Me Not on the Lone Prairie." I structured the song like a formal cowboy's lament, borrowing and adapting the tunes from "The Streets of Laredo" and "Git Along, Little Dogies."

When introducing the song to children, pull out cowboy books like *Songs of the Wild West* to show pictures of cowpunchers, and be sure to define unfamiliar words like *lamentations, alas, alack,* and *beseech.*

Children of all ages need a gentle reminder at least once a year about how to care for their books. Pulling some grievously injured patients off the shelf of our Book Hospital, acting out my role as Book Doctor, I engage classes in spirited debate over how we can keep our books healthy. "Alas and Alack" allows me to bring up the subject with older children without pestering them. They find the song amusingly sad and continue to alert us to book emergencies when they take out a book with a sagging spine in need of glue or a cover begging for a new plastic dust jacket.

Watch your children turn the pages of their library books, and you'll realize that some of them have never been taught how to do it correctly. It's never too late to demonstrate proper technique. Show them a book with rips along the bottom of the page to bring home the fact that every time a reader turns the page from the bottom it weakens the paper. Tiny tears will grow larger and larger and become big rips if not mended. My kindergartners learn the page-turning chant, "Squeeze, Slide, Push," as they gently squeeze the corner of the page, slide their hand under the whole page, and carefully push it over.

Have children been turning the book over face down or dog-earing the corner instead of using a bookmark? Vocalize your horror at that kind of treatment, and you'll hear from parents who say, "My son yelled at me when I put my book down. He ran and got me a bookmark!"

Why is this important? Children who learn from adults to respect books and handle them with deference will be more likely to value reading and will pass that love onto their own children in time.

Alas and Alack: The Wounded Book's Lament

Words by Judy Freeman, ©1991

Music traditional

As I was a-walk-ing the hall-ways of
my school, I spied the li-brar-y, the door o-pen
wide; I stopped in to browse, take a look at some
fic-tion, when one of the vol-umes cried out from inside. A-las, a-lack, please don't hurt me or
bruise me, Don't cray-on my pag-es or

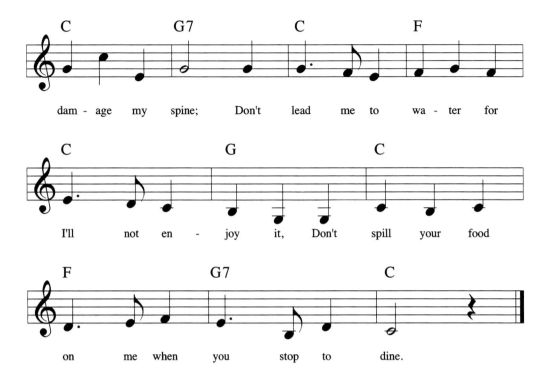

dam - age my spine; Don't lead me to wa - ter for

I'll not en - joy it, Don't spill your food

on me when you stop to dine.

Note: The accompanying recording is in the key of C sharp.

Children's Books to Use with "Alas and Alack: The Wounded Book's Lament"

Baker, Alan. ***Benjamin's Book***. Illus. by the author. Lothrop, 1982. OP; unp.; Grades PreK–1)

Hamster Benjamin makes a mark on the nice clean page with his dirty pawprint, and then he makes things worse by trying to clean it up.

Johnston, Tony. ***The Cowboy and the Black-Eyed Pea***. Illus. by Warren Ludwig. Putnam, 1992. (ISBN 0-399-22330-4; unp.; Grades 1–4)

In an Old West retelling of Hans Christian Andersen's familiar princess tale, Texas heiress Farethee Well, looking for a real cowboy who will love her for herself, comes up with a test to find someone sensitive enough to feel a pea hidden under a pile of saddle blankets atop a horse.

Porte, Barbara Ann. ***Harry in Trouble***. Illus. by Yossi Abolafia. Greenwillow, 1989. (ISBN 0-688-07722-6; unp.; Grades K–2)

It's the third time Harry's library card has disappeared, and he musters up the courage to tell his librarian, Ms. Katz, just how it happened.

Sadler, Marilyn. ***Alistair in Outer Space***. Illus. by Roger Bollen. Prentice-Hall, 1984. (ISBN 0-671-68504-X; unp.; Grades K–2)

Nerdy genius Alistair Grittle is so focused on returning his books to the library that being shanghaied by a Gootulan spaceship only strengthens his resolve to get back before the books are late.

Scieszka, Jon. *The Book That Jack Wrote.* Illus. by Daniel Adel. Viking, 1994. (ISBN 0-670-84330-X; unp.; Grades 1–4)

Told in "The House That Jack Built" style, this surreal nursery rhyme parody follows a book, rat, cat, dog, cow, humming baby, and flying pie, all leading back to smug, bespectacled Jack.

Songs of the Wild West. Commentary by Alan Axelrod. Arrangements by Dan Fox. Simon & Schuster, 1991. (ISBN 0-671-74775-4; 128p.; Grades 2–6)

A magnificent compilation of 45 folk songs about cowboys, outlaws, railroaders, and Westward travelers, accompanied by reproductions of paintings and other artwork from the Metropolitan Museum of Art in New York.

Teague, Mark. *How I Spent My Summer Vacation.* Illus. by the author. Crown, 1996. (ISBN 0-517-59998-8; unp.; Grades K–3)

Student Wallace Bleff regales his teacher and classmates with his wild rhyming saga of how, en route to visit his Aunt Fern out West, he was captured by cowboys and carried off to their cow camp for the summer.

Turner, Priscilla. *The War Between the Vowels and the Consonants.* Illus. by Whitney Turner. Farrar, 1996. (ISBN 0-374-28236-0; unp.; Grades 1–5)

After their taunts and threats lead to war, the rival vowels and consonants must unite to defeat a greater foe, a jagged scribble of chaos that cannot withstand the letters' power when they form their first word: "STOP."

The Biggest Book

Grade Level: 2–6

As I went to the library, it was on library day,
I spied the biggest book, sir, just standing on display.

CHORUS:
    Well it's true, my lad, it's true, my lad, I never was known to lie.
    And if you go to the library, you'll see the same as I.

The pages in this book, sir, they reached up to the moon;
I started it in January, didn't finish till June.
CHORUS

The print inside this book, sir, was tiny beyond hope;
To read a single page, sir, you'd need a microscope.
CHORUS

The cover of this book, sir, it reached up to the sky;
The eagles built a nest in it, you could hear the young ones cry.
CHORUS

The text inside this book, sir, was wild beyond belicf;
I wiped my brow a thousand times with a nine-foot handkerchief.
CHORUS

The pictures in this book, sir, they leaped right off the page;
I caught them as they came to life and placed them in a cage.
CHORUS

The author of this book, sir, was mighty rich and fine,
But not so much a liar as the singer of these lines.
CHORUS

The Biggest Book

Words by Judy Freeman, ©1989; to the tune of "The Darby Ram"

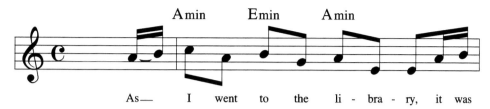

As— I went to the li - bra - ry, it was

on li - bra - ry day, I— spied the big - gest book,— sir, just

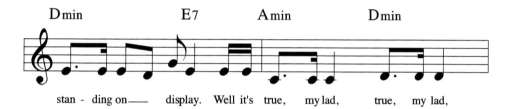

stan - ding on— display. Well it's true, my lad, true, my lad,

I ne - ver was known to lie. And if you go to the li - bra - ry, you'll

see the same as I— .

CHILDREN OFTEN DO NOT UNDERSTAND THE HUMOR IN tall tales. Tall tales sound sensible because they are told or read with a straight face, and children can't tell they're supposed to be off-the-wall funny. Too often second-grade teachers will attempt a tall-tale unit and wonder why it seems so dry. Until kids develop their sense of irony, sometime after third grade, they don't understand this type of humor and it may seem stupid to them.

We need to present children with broad exaggerations that they can visualize. The old English folk song "The Darby Ram" does just that, and I "borrowed" the song's structure, its chorus, and a few of the verses and transposed it into a tall tale about books. Now that picture books come out in "Big Book" editions, perhaps the song is not so far-fetched.

Start them thinking: "The book was so wide / high / fat / hard to read / funny that . . . ." Have them brainstorm exaggerations, and see if they can write new verses to the song.

Children's Books to Use with "The Biggest Book"

Day, David. *The Sleeper.* Illus. by Mark Entwhistle. Ideals, 1990. (ISBN 0-8249-8456-0; unp.; Grades 2–4)

After Emperor Chin the Merciless decrees all libraries in China must be emptied, young monk Wu is entrusted with delivering the most valuable books to the emperor. Instead he falls into a deep sleep for 200 years, awakening with his books intact just in time to stop an impending battle and bring peace to the land.

Drescher, Henrik. *Simon's Book.* Illus. by the author. Lothrop, 1983. (ISBN 0-688-02086-0; unp.; Grades K–2)

A young boy draws a story about Simon and a scary monster, and when he falls asleep his pens and the pictures on the page come to life—including the monster.

Fleischman, Sid. *McBroom Tells the Truth.* Illus. by Walter H. Lorraine, Little, Brown, 1981. (ISBN 0-316-28550-1; 48 p.; Grades 2–5)

Down on Josh McBroom's wondrous one-acre farm, crops grow in a single day, which delights his brood of children, named Will*jill*hester*chester*peter*polly*tim-*tom*mary*larry*andlittle*clarina*, but aggra-

vates his skinflint neighbor, Heck Jones, in a literary tall tale that is a model of a straight-faced string of whoppers.

Green, John F. *Alice and the Birthday Giant.* Illus. by Maryann Kovalski. Scholastic, 1989. (ISBN 0-590-43428-4; unp.; Grades K–3)

On her birthday Alice finds a one-eyed giant in her bedroom. When she can't figure out how to send him home, she consults Ms. McCracken, the librarian, who locates the perfect book of magic spells.

Haley, Gail E. *Dream Peddler.* Illus. by the author. Dutton, 1993. (ISBN 0-525-45153-6; unp.; Grades 1–5)

Poor, itinerant book peddler John Chapman receives a message in a dream telling him that a visit to London Bridge will bring him great joy, which it does in a roundabout way.

Hodges, Margaret. *Saint Patrick and the Peddler.* Illus. by Paul Brett Johnson. Orchard, 1993. (ISBN 0-531-08639-9; unp.; Grades 1–4)

A poor Irish peddler learns to read the writing on his porridge pot after he dreams that Saint Patrick tells him to go to a

Dublin bridge where he will hear a good thing. Pair this with Gail E. Haley's *Dream Peddler* above and compare the two variants.

Isaacs, Anne. *Swamp Angel*. Illus. by Paul O. Zelinsky. Dutton, 1994. (ISBN 0-525-45271-0; unp.; Grades 1–4)

In a gorgeously illustrated Caldecott Honor Medal picture book, a 19th-century tall-tale giantess, the "greatest woodswoman in Tennessee," commences a five-day wrestling match with gargantuan bear Thundering Tarnation to earn the moniker "Champion Wildcat."

Polacco, Patricia. *Aunt Chip and the Great Triple Creek Dam Affair*. Illus. by the author. Philomel, 1996. (ISBN 0-399-22943-4; unp.; Grades 1–4)

Eli's Aunt Charlotte is the only person in the TV-fixated town of Triple Creek who remembers how to read, and when Eli learns, too, he amazes all the children in town by reading to them. Polacco's valuable message of turning off the doggone TV and curling up with a good book borrowed from that safe haven of knowledge, the library, will hit home. Share this as a kickoff to "No TV Week" or just to get kids thinking about why they read.

Scieszka, Jon. *The Stinky Cheese Man and Other Fairly Stupid Tales*. Illus. by Lane Smith. Viking, 1992. (ISBN 0-670-84487-X; unp.; Grades 1–6)

In one of the great and hilarious folk- and fairy-tale parodies of our time, we meet up with outrageous characters, including Little Red Running Shorts, the Really Ugly Duckling, and Cinderumpelstiltskin.

Stevenson, James. *Brrr!* Illus. by the author. Greenwillow, 1991. (ISBN 0-688-09211-X; unp.; Grades K–2)

Grandpa regales grandkids Mary Ann and Louie with another "true" tall tale from his boyhood about the extraordinary winter of 1908, when the snow came down so hard it covered the entire town.

Teague, Mark. *Frog Medicine*. Illus. by the author. Scholastic, 1991. (ISBN 0-590-44177-9; unp.; Grades 1–4)

Unwilling to read an assigned book for school, Elmo procrastinates. On the morning his book report is due, he is horrified to discover his feet have grown long, slimy, and green.

Wood, Audrey. *The Bunyans*. Illus. by David Shannon. Blue Sky/Scholastic, 1996. (ISBN 0-590-48089-8; unp.; Grades 1–5)

Although you may have heard tales about Paul Bunyan and his blue ox, Babe, this entertaining picture book lets you know about the tall-tale antics of the rest of Paul's giant family: wife Carrie, who dug out Mammoth Cave in Kentucky, and kids Little Jean and Teeny. Use a map to point out the locations of all the natural wonders the family purportedly created.

Look for 398.2

A chant by Judy Freeman, ©1983
Grade Level: K–3

If you want a good story, let me tell you what to do—
Look for 398.2, look for 398.2!

Prince or princess in hot water, trouble with a witch's brew—
Look for 398.2, look for 398.2!

Fierce and fire-breathing dragons, shiny scales of green and
  blue—
Look for 398.2, look for 398.2!

Ogres, leprechauns, and goblins all are waiting just for you—
Look for 398.2, look for 398.2!

Find a tale from every country, from Australia to Peru—
Look for 398.2, look for 398.2!

That's all you've gotta do.

USE THIS CHANT TO INTRODUCE CHILDREN TO ONE OF THE most enjoyable areas of the library, the folk- and fairy-tale section, or the 398s. These books have stories ranging back hundreds and sometimes thousands of years, to the old "once-upon-a-time" days.

"Why aren't these books in the fiction section if they're made-up stories?" children ask.

That's a tough question, especially when children learn that nonfiction books are true. Along with joke books and poetry, folklore is another exception to that rule. Folklore belongs in the 300s, with the social science books that explain how people live, what families do, and how people's lives are organized. They give us a window on people's beliefs, customs, and struggles across the globe.

We don't know who first composed folk and fairy tales. As with nursery rhymes, the authors have been lost to history as stories were passed verbally from generation to generation, village to village, and country to country. Such famous names in folklore as the Brothers Grimm, Charles Perrault, and P. C. Asbjørnsen were collectors and retellers of stories and not the stories' original composers. Check the cover of many folktale books, and you'll see the words "Retold by" in front of the author's name.

I have listeners snap their fingers in time to the rhythm of the chant and then join in on the second "Look for 398.2" refrain for each verse. Sometimes I'll divide the group into four, with the first section yelling out, "Three!" the second, "Ninety-eight!" the third, "Point!" and the last, "Two." One result of all this yelling is that every student in my school can tell you "Miss Freeman's favorite number," and fairy tales are a visible and well-loved part of our library book collection.

To go along with the chant, select a batch of memorable folktales that exemplify each element of the poem—princes, princesses, witches, dragons, ogres, leprechauns, goblins—and read aloud or booktalk each title. Or booktalk international tales, one from each of six continents (leaving out Antarctica, of course, as penguins

don't tell stories), or ones from different regions of the United States. Children will not realize the wealth of stories abounding in the library's folklore section until you begin to do some publicizing. The following list of a few of my particular favorites will get you started.

Children's Books to Use with "Look For 398.2"

Arranged to correspond with characters mentioned in the chant.

FOR A COMPREHENSIVE LISTING OF BOOKS, SEE THE "FOLK & FAIRY TALES, MYTHS & LEGENDS" CHAPTERS OF BOOKS KIDS WILL SIT STILL FOR (BOWKER, 1990) AND MORE BOOKS KIDS WILL SIT STILL FOR (BOWKER, 1995)

"Prince or princess in hot water"

Kimmel, Eric A. *The Three Princes: A Tale from the Middle East.* Illus. by Leonard Everett Fisher. Holiday House, 1994. (ISBN 0-8234-1115-X; unp.; Grades 1–4)

Determined to marry Prince Mohsen, the man she loves, a princess sends him and two other suitors on a year-long quest, saying she will marry the man who brings back the greatest wonder.

"Trouble with a witch's brew"

DePaola, Tomie. *Strega Nona.* Illus. by the author. Simon & Schuster, 1979. (ISBN 0-671-66283-X; unp.; Grades K–4)

"Don't touch the pasta pot," Strega Nona admonishes her hapless new assistant, Big Anthony, before she leaves town. But of course he never listens, and before you know it the Italian village is overflowing with pasta.

"Fierce and fire-breathing dragons"

Lawson, Julie. *The Dragon's Pearl.* Illus. by Paul Morin. Clarion, 1993. (ISBN 0-395-63623-X; unp.; Grades 1–4)

Finding a magic pearl at first brings good fortune to Xiao Sheng and his mother. But when ruffians threaten to steal the pearl, the boy swallows it and is transformed into a dragon who ends the drought in his Chinese province of Szechwan.

"Ogres"

Kirstein, Lincoln. *Puss in Boots.* Illus. by Alain Vaïs. Little, Brown, 1992. (ISBN 0-316-89506-7; unp.; Grades 1–4)

The sumptuous paintings in this splendid version of the folktale about a cat who defeats an ogre and makes Robin, his poor young master, a rich man will give you the feeling you've just visited the château country of France.

"Leprechauns"

Shute, Linda. *Clever Tom and the Leprechaun.* Illus. by the author. Lothrop, 1988. (ISBN 0-688-07488-X; unp.; Grades PreK–3)

When Tom stumbles upon a leprechaun, he tries hard not to be tricked by the wee little man before he finds out where his buried treasure is hidden.

"Goblins"

McCoy, Karen Kawamoto. *A Tale of Two Tengu: A Japanese Folktale.* Illus. by Ken Fossey. Albert Whitman, 1993. (ISBN 0-8075-7748-0; unp.; Grades PreK–2)

Kenji and Joji, two Japanese tengu (mountain-dwelling goblins with long, lovely noses) compete to see who can snare the best prize by sending their noses stretching for miles.

A Sampling of One Appealing Tale from Each Continent (Except Antarctica)

"Find a tale from every country, from Australia to Peru . . ."

Africa

Aardema, Verna. *Misoso: Once Upon a Time Tales from Africa*. Illus. by Reynold Ruffins. Apple Soup/Knopf, 1994. (ISBN 0-679-83430-3; 88p.; Grades 2–6)

There are 12 beguiling folktales from 11 African countries in this attractive and tellable collection.

Asia

Han, Suzanne Crowder. *The Rabbit's Escape*. Illus. by Yumi Heo. Henry Holt, 1995. (ISBN 0-8050-2675-4; unp.; Grades 1–5)

When the Dragon King of the East Sea becomes ill, he seeks help from a fast-talking rabbit whose fresh raw liver is the only cure. As in similar tales from the United States and Africa, this Korean folktale features a trickster rabbit who talks his way out of trouble.

Australia

Czernecki, Stefan, and Timothy Rhodes. *The Singing Snake*. Illus. by Stefan Czernecki. Hyperion, 1993. (ISBN 1-56282-400-7; unp.; Grades K–2)

In this Australian pourquoi tale about the first flute, Old Man promises to make a musical instrument to honor the creature who sings the best, and Snake wins by deception.

Europe

Sanderson, Ruth. *Papa Gatto: An Italian Fairy Tale*. Illus. by the author. Little, Brown, 1995. (ISBN 0-316-77073-6; unp.; Grades 1–5)

Lush, sumptuous, Renaissance-style paintings accompany this tale of two sisters— one, lovely, lazy, and coldhearted; the other, plain but kind and hardworking— who both apply for a job looking after the kittens of widower cat Papa Gatto, the prince's adviser.

North America

Hooks, William. *Moss Gown*. Illus. by Donald Carrick. Clarion, 1987. (ISBN 0-89919-460-5; unp.; Grades 2–6)

In a Cinderella variant set in the southern United States, youngest daughter Candace is banished from her plantation home after she tells her beloved father that she loves him more than meat loves salt and her sisters deliberately misinterpret her analogy.

Cohn, Amy L. *From Sea to Shining Sea: A Treasury of American Folklore and Folk Songs*. Illus. by 11 Caldecott Medal and 4 Caldecott Honor book artists. Scholastic, 1993. (ISBN 0-590-42868-3; 399p.; Grades 1–6)

With an assortment of stories, poems, songs, and other Americana, ranging from tall tales and ghost stories to historical events and ethnic tales, and an array of colorful and handsome illustrations by Caldecott award-winning artists, this masterful compilation encompasses the history of the United States through its folklore.

South America

Ehlert, Lois. *Moon Rope: Un Lazo a la Luna: A Peruvian Folktale*. Illus. by the author. Harcourt, 1992. (ISBN 0-15-255343-6; unp.; Grades PreK–2)

More than anything, Mole would like to go to the moon, so Fox braids a grass rope that he convinces the birds to hitch to the moon's tip, and the two begin their climb.

More Fun with Folklore

Bernstein, Joanne E., and Paul Cohen. ***What Was the Wicked Witch's Real Name? And Other Character Riddles.*** Illus. by Ann Iosa. Albert Whitman, 1986. (ISBN 0-8075-8854-7; unp.; Grades 2–6)

Dozens upon dozens of groaners take off folklore, Mother Goose, literature, TV, and the funnies.

Walton, Rick, and Ann Walton. ***Kiss a Frog! Jokes About Fairy Tales, Knights, and Dragons.*** Illus. by Joan Hanson. Lerner, 1989. (ISBN 0-8225-0970-9; unp.; Grades PreK–4)

This minibook from the kid-centered Make Me Laugh series includes plenty of word-play puns on Cinderella, Sleeping Beauty, and other mainstream fairy tales.

Chapter 2

Throw It Out the Window

All About Nonsense

CHILDREN LEARNING TO NAVIGATE THROUGH THE INTRICA-cies of the English language need time to play with words. Often they misunderstand what they hear, making their own particular sense out of an idiomatic expression. In my library, when a child wants me to hold a book for him, I put it on the "Save Shelf" until he can come in to pick it up. Invariably, kindergartners ask me to put their books on the "safety shelf."

Misunderstandings are not limited to young children either. At the beginning of the school year, my cousin Farrell Fand, English teacher at Maplewood Middle School in New Jersey, asks his seventh-grade students to write their autobiographies, telling them he will be good enough to supply the paper.

"I don't want to be unreasonable," he tells them. "Tell me what I need to find out so I can get to know you. Leave out unimportant stuff because the paper is on the small side." He then hands each student a 1" x 2" card, adding, "Don't worry. You can use both sides."

One year, reading through their miniature narratives, he came across a statement that puzzled him for a moment. A boy had written, "I am lack toast and tolerant."

The next day, Farrell said to the student, "I read your autobiography. There's something I should clear up. Is it true you can't have any milk products?"

"Yeah," said the boy. "I get real sick if I do."

Several years back, Farrell assigned vocabulary words that students had to write in a sentence. For "decrepit," one boy wrote, "The cat decrepit up on the mouse."

Ask your students if they've ever misunderstood a common phrase, and you'll come up with an interesting and funny list too.

Paul Levitt, coauthor of *The Weighty Word Book* and English professor at the University of Colorado at Boulder, is concerned about three major deficiencies in college students today: an inability to read closely, poor writing skills, and a "desperate paucity of vocabulary."

He described one conversation in a class where he asked if anyone was familiar with Shaw's *Pygmalion*. "I've totally heard of it," replied one young woman in typical college-speak.

"Totally? That's good. That must mean we can discuss the play."

"No," she replied, alarmed. "I don't know anything about it. I've just heard it mentioned a lot."

Paul tells his students, "You are going to spend the rest of your lives in one place and one place only—in your head. So you had better furnish it richly, for you will live in that vast and wonderful world you have created. The experiences you are having now are the foundation—the smells, the memories—of your lives. You will in the future draw on the things you have experienced in the past."

Paul says, "Words are powerful magic. A bad word can get you in trouble—the sky can fall. A beautiful word is poetry. Just a little sound can change the way you feel. If language has that kind of power, then certainly you want to harness it."

The songs in this chapter rely on puns, wordplay, incongruities, and silly situations that in their own giddy way lead to an infatuation with language. Many are old camp songs or folk songs that have been rattling around the United States a long time. Folklore is filled with marvelous bits of nonsense too good not to try aloud. As with tall tales, children need to be introduced to nonsense as an art form, because they can be so literal and often don't know what to make of such silliness.

Once you've made it clear to your children that you approve of and appreciate good wordplay, they won't let you down.

"Spaghetti," I said to second grader Erin, pointing to her perpetually untied sneakers, laces lapping the ground. Somehow, saying "spaghetti" entices my kids into tying their shoes quicker than regular nagging.

She looked down, shrugged, and grinned. "But Miss Freeman," she said, "I'm not allowed to play with my food!"

Touché!

Throw It Out the Window

Grade Level: PreK–2

Old Mother Hubbard went to the cupboard
to fetch her poor dog a bone;
But when she got there, the cupboard was bare,
So she threw it out the window, the window,
the second-story window;
But when she got there, the cupboard was bare,
So she threw it out the window.

Little Miss Muffett sat on her tuffet,
eating her curds and whey;
Along came a spider and sat down beside her,
And she threw it out the window, the window,
the second-story window;
Along came a spider and sat down beside her,
And threw it out the window.

Humpty Dumpty sat on a wall,
Humpty Dumpty had a great fall;
All the king's horses and all the king's men,
They threw him out the window, the window,
the second-story window;
All the king's horses and all the king's men,
They threw him out the window.

Other Verses

Old King Cole / Jack and Jill / Little Bo Peep / Yankee Doodle

Throw It Out the Window

Traditional

Old Moth-er Hub-bard went to the cupboard to fetch her poor dog a

bone. But when she got there, the cup-board was bare, so she

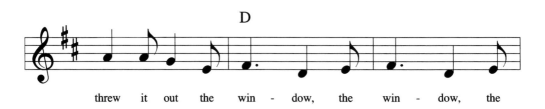

threw it out the win - dow, the win - dow, the

sec - ond sto - ry win - dow, But when she got there, the

cup-board was bare, So she threw it out the win - dow.

I CAN'T GUARANTEE WHAT YOUR CHILDREN'S REACTIONS TO this song will be. My kindergartners find it so hilarious they roll around on the floor every time we get to the chorus. But when my nephew Josh first heard this song, at the tender age of two and one-half, he was outraged. "Don't throw it out the window!" he shrieked, alarmed, when I came to the chorus. Obviously, some children take their nursery rhymes seriously and want to see them treated with respect. Older preschoolers get their first taste of parody and anarchy with this song, and they appreciate it greatly.

When I ask my kindergartners to supply additional verses they know, someone always raises a hand and says, "Mother Goose." I then explain that all of the rhymes we fool with in the song are called Mother Goose nursery rhymes, and I ask them to keep thinking of others. For all children, this is an easy, if slightly cynical, way of reviewing the standard nursery rhymes—although not every rhyme works; "Three Blind Mice" and "There Was an Old Woman Who Lived in a Shoe," for instance, are too long or awkward to sing.

Afterward, make available to them several good Mother Goose collections, such as those listed below.

Children's Books to Use with "Throw It Out the Window"

SEE ALSO BOOKS LISTED UNDER "AIN'T WE CRAZY?" PAGE 89.

Ada, Alma Flor. *Dear Peter Rabbit.* Illus. by Leslie Tryon. Atheneum, 1994. (ISBN 0-689-31850-2; unp.; Grades K–2)

As we ascertain from a series of letters that one folktale character writes to another, the Big Bad Wolf blows down two houses, threatens Red Riding Hood, and loses his tail, while the Three Bears, Peter Rabbit, Little Red Riding Hood, and the Three Little Pigs get together for Goldilocks's birthday party.

Ahlberg, Janet, and Allan Ahlberg. *Each Peach Pear Plum: An 'I Spy' Story.* Illus. by the authors. Viking, 1979. (ISBN 0-670-28705-9; unp.; Grades PreK–K)

Follow the directions of each simple rhyming couplet and identify the folktale or nursery rhyme character hiding in the whimsical illustration on the facing page.

DePaola, Tomie. *The Comic Adventures of Old Mother Hubbard and Her Dog.* Illus. by the author. Harcourt, 1981. (ISBN 0-15-219541-6; unp.; Grades PreK–1)

The complete version of the English nursery rhyme, detailing what happened after the old woman set out to fill her bare cupboard. This one's great fun to act out.

DePaola, Tomie, comp. *Tomie dePaola's Mother Goose.* Illus. by Tomie dePaola. Putnam, 1985. (ISBN 0-399-21258-2; 127p.; Grades PreK–2)

There are almost 200 rhymes in this oversized collection, with dePaola's trademark paintings, all pastel and cheery.

Foreman, Michael, comp. *Michael Foreman's Mother Goose.* Illus. by Michael Foreman. Harcourt, 1991. (ISBN 0-15-255820-9; 158p.; Grades PreK–2)

Foreman's soft, lovely watercolors accompany this stately collection, with rhymes grouped by subject and type, and complete verses for "Jack and Jill," "Simple Simon," "Cock Robin," and "London Bridge Is Falling Down."

Glazer, Tom, comp. *The Mother Goose Songbook*. Illus. by David McPhail. Doubleday, 1990. (ISBN 0-385-41474-9; 96p.; Grades PreK–2)

Forty-four familiar rhymes are all set to music, some with tunes composed and new verses added by folksinger Glazer, and each score is illustrated with large, attractive watercolors.

Lobel, Arnold, comp. *The Random House Book of Mother Goose*. Illus. by Arnold Lobel. Random House, 1986. (ISBN 0-394-86799-8; 176p.; Grades PreK–2)

Another must-have collection, with 300-plus rhymes and Lobel's enticing and colorful illustrations on every page.

Marshall, James, comp. *James Marshall's Mother Goose*. Illus. by James Marshall. Farrar, 1979. (ISBN 0-374-33653-9; unp.; Grades PreK–2)

Marshall's usual assortment of goofy dogs, mice, pigs, and chickens romp through three dozen nursery rhymes.

Marshall, James. *Old Mother Hubbard and Her Wonderful Dog*. Illus. by the author. Farrar, 1991. (ISBN 0-374-35621-1; unp.; Grades PreK–1)

Rats, cats, and chickens run riot in the background while the feisty bulldog plays dead, dances, and reads the news in this Mother Goose rhyme, always perfect for creative dramatics.

Opie, Iona, ed. *My Very First Mother Goose*. Illus. by Rosemary Wells. Candlewick, 1996. (ISBN 1-56402-620-5; 108p., Grades PreK–2)

Children who adore Wells's charming animal characters will be entranced with her oversized and captivating illustrations for this assortment of 60 well-loved rhymes.

Opie, Iona, and Peter Opie, eds. *Tail Feathers from Mother Goose: The Opie Rhyme Book*. Little. Brown, 1988. (ISBN 0-316-65081-1; 124p.; Grades PreK–3)

The more than 60 rhymes collected here are almost all previously unpublished and include different versions of well-known rhymes, all spectacularly illustrated by 60 familiar artists, most of them English.

Polette, Nancy. *The Hole by the Apple Tree: An A–Z Discovery Tale*. Illus. by Nishan Akgulian. Greenwillow, 1992. (ISBN 0-688-10558-0; unp.; Grades K–2)

As he digs a hole by the Apple tree, Harold explains to his friends that he is planting Beans to make a beanstalk grow up to the Castle, so he can meet a Giant, Monster, and other alphabetical fairy-tale characters.

Sutherland, Zena, comp. *The Orchard Book of Nursery Rhymes*. Illus. by Faith Jaques. Orchard, 1990. (ISBN 0-531-05903-0; 88p.; Grades PreK–1)

This standout collection of 77 nursery rhymes boasts large, luxurious pages decorated with delicate late-18th-century-style watercolors.

Tolhurst, Marilyn. *Somebody and the Three Blairs*. Illus. by Simone Abel. Orchard, 1991. (ISBN 0-531-08478-7; unp.; Grades PreK–1)

In this gentle parody, Mr. and Mrs. and Baby Blair head off for a walk in the park, and Somebody, in the form of a friendly-looking large brown bear, stops in to taste the cereal, try out the chairs, play in the kitchen, investigate the bathroom, and check out the beds.

Yolen, Jane, comp. *Jane Yolen's Mother Goose Songbook*. Illus. by Rosekrans Hoffman. Musical arrangement by Adam Stemple. Caroline House/Boyds Mills, 1992. (ISBN 1-878093-52-5; 95p.; Grades PreK–2)

Sing your way through this collection of 49 songs, with music, chords, and whimsical, lavish, colored-ink illustrations.

Prinderella and the Cince

As cranstribed by Alice H. Yucht, ©1992
Grade Level: 3–6

Tonce upon a wime there lived a gritty little pearl named Prinderella. She lived in a hovely louse with her stugly sep-isters and her sticked wep-mother. All lay dong Prinderella had to do all the hork of the wousehold; wean the clindows, flub the scroor, pine the shots and shans, and do all the other wirty dirk, while her sugly isters and sticked wep-mother dept all slay on beather feds. Prinderella was treated bery vadly and had to wear roppy slags that fidn't dit. Isn't that a shirty dame?

Done way, the Quing and Keen prade a moclamation that there would be a brand drancy-fess gall in honor of the Cince, and all the geligible irls of the kole whingdom were invited. So the kole whing-dom prepared for the brand gall. Prinderella's stugly sep-isters and sticked wep-mother made Prinderella murk all day to wake their drancy fesses.

Then poor Prinderella, in her roppy slags that fidn't dit, had to hay stome as her sugly isters and sticked wep-mother went off to the brand gall in a covely larriage. Wasn't that a shirty dame!

Prinderella dat in the soorway, crobbing and sying till her gairy fodmother, who lived in a laraway fand, heard her and came to see mat was the whatter.

"Oh! Gairy Fodmother," cried Prinderella, "I feel so serribly tad! Why can't I bo to the gall and pree the Cince?"

"Near fot, chy mild. You SHALL bo to the gall!" said the gairy fodmother. "Now, so to the geller and bring me some pice, a mumpkin, and three rat fats."

When Prinderella brought the pice, the mumpkin, and the rat fats, the gairy fodmother fapped her sningers, touched them with her wagic mand, and changed the mumpkin into a hoach, the pice into corses, and the rat fats into moachcen.

But Prinderella still had nothing to wear but roppy slags that fidn't dit. Wasn't that a shirty dame? So the gairy fodmother quickly fapped her sningers again, winkled her tye, and there was a garkling spown of gilver and sold, all covered with pubies and rearls. It was the bost dreautiful mess in the kole whingdom! And for her feet, there was a painty dair of slass glippers.

As the gairy fodmother clelped Prinderella himb into the covely larriage, she warned her: "Don't gorfet: you must beave lefore the moke of stridnight, for the brell will be spoken when the twock clikes strelve."

Prinderella was the bost meautiful baiden at the mall. When the Cince saw her fovely lace and her dreautiful bess all covered with pubies and rearls, he lell in fove with her. They nanced all dight, until the calace plock chegan to bime. Then, just before the last moke of stridnight, Prinderella dan out the roor to her waiting harriage and courses. But as she durried hown the stalace peps, she slopped her dripper! Now wasn't that a shirty dame?

The dext nay, the Ping issued a kroclamation that the Cince was lesperately dooking for the meautiful baiden who had slopped her dripper as she left the brand gall. The Cince hent to the wouses of all the geligible irls of the kole whingdom in gearch of the sirl he had lallen in fove with, and now manted to warry. When the Cince came to Prinderella's house, her stugly sep-isters all tried to tit their foes into the slass glipper, but it fidn't dit!

But whuess gat? When Prinderella flipped her soot into the slass glipper, it fid dit! So Prinderella and the Cince mere warried. She wore a gedding wown of wharkling spite, all covered with pubies and rearls. And Prinderella and the Cince hived lappily ever after. That wasn't such a shirty dame, was it?

THOUGH FRIENDS TELL ME THERE IS ANOTHER VERSION OF Prinderella told by humorist Richard Lederer, this one is based on several versions as told by New Jersey folks Carol Phillips, head of Children's Services at East Brunswick Public Library (who recited the entire story from memory during one memorable and riotous storytellers' get-together many years back); Betty Butler, formerly the reading teacher at Joyce Kilmer Middle School in Milltown; and children's literature consultant, author, and librarian Alice Yucht, who collated the several versions into this one.

When you introduce the story, start by announcing you've heard lots of good fairy tales in your time, like "Wo Snite and the Deven Swarves" and "Beeping Sleauty." Oh, yes, and don't forget "The Pree Thittle Ligs" and "Gransel and Hetel!"

At this point, your students will either be laughing hysterically or looking at you like you've got a major screw loose. As some students catch on, they'll start translating the titles for others: "She means Hansel and Gretel!"

Keep going. You want to make sure they have the idea before you launch into your reading of "Prinderella" so they have a fair chance of understanding the humor of the story that comes from transposing initial consonants.

"Now let me think. There's also 'Back and the Jeanstalk' and the 'Bee Thrilly Groats Guff,' 'Buss in Poots,' and, of course, everybody's favorite, 'Prinderella and the Cince.'"

If your students are savvy, at about this time they'll figure out how you're messing up those fairy-tale titles and perhaps start to volunteer others. That's when you begin your reading. With fourth and fifth graders, read the story the first time and watch them howl over "Wasn't that a shirty dame" and that wonderful dress with all the "pubies and rearls." Don't be surprised when some of the phrases become classroom expressions: "Whuess gat!" or "Near fot, chy mild!" for starters.

Read the story a second time, after handing out the text to every child so they can follow as you read. Then let them try to read it aloud, once they've figured out how it all works, with all of those switched consonants. Define this speech oddity, telling them about spoonerisms, named after William Spooner (1844–1930), an English clergyman and warden of Oxford University's New College, who came out with unintentionally funny statements such as "Our next hymn will be Kinkering Congs."

This is a delightful story to record. Let each student take a sentence, or cast parts and have them act it out as Reader's Theater. Encourage them to take the story home and try it out on their parents. Pair up children and have them rewrite another tale in the same vein. Read a compendium of Cinderella stories and parodies, several of which are listed below. Above all, have a lot of laughs. That's not such a shirty dame, is it?

Children's Books to Use with "Prinderella and the Cince"

SEE ALSO BOOKS LISTED UNDER "AIN'T WE CRAZY?" PAGE 89.

Agee, Jon. *Go Hang a Salami! I'm a Lasagna Hog! And Other Palindromes.* Illus. by the author. Farrar, 1992. (ISBN 0-374-33473-0; unp.; Grades 2–6)

"Yo, Bozo Boy" is just one of the more than 60 clever palindromes, each illustrated with an amusing pen-and-ink line drawing. Also search out the companion book *So Many Dynamos! and Other Palindromes* (1994).

Climo, Shirley. *The Egyptian Cinderella.* Illus. by Ruth Heller. Crowell, 1989. (ISBN 0-690-04824-6; unp.; Grades 2–6)

Stolen from her home in Greece and sold as a slave in Egypt, lovely Rhodopis loses one of her leather and gold slippers, a gift from her master, when a falcon steals it and drops it in the lap of the Pharaoh.

Jackson, Ellen. *Cinder Edna.* Illus. by Kevin O'Malley. Lothrop, 1994. (ISBN 0-688-12323-6; unp.; Grades 2–6)

Cinderella's next-door neighbor, take-charge, resourceful Edna, takes the bus to the ball, finds Prince Charming "borrrrring," and hits it off with his socially conscious younger brother Rupert.

Karlin, Barbara. *Cinderella.* Illus. by James Marshall. Little, Brown, 1989. (ISBN 0-316-54654-2; unp.; Grades PreK–2)

What makes this simple retelling of the folktale so delightful is Marshall's genially daffy illustrations, which match perfectly the mood of "Prinderella and the Cince."

Kaye, M. M. *The Ordinary Princess.* Doubleday, 1984. (ISBN 0-671-60383-3; 112p.; Grades 3–5)

At the christening of Princess Amy, the seventh princess born to the King and Queen, Fairy Crustacea's gift is that the child will be "ordinary." An appreciative Princess Amy rejects the royal life-style, runs away, and becomes a kitchen maid.

Minters, Frances. *Cinder-Elly.* Illus. by G. Brian Karas. Viking, 1993. (ISBN 0-670-84417-9; unp.; Grades 1–3)

In snappy, rap-style rhyme, we are introduced to a hard-cleaning New York City girl whose two sisters head off to a basketball game, a magical godmother, and that famous basketball star Prince Charming.

Myers, Bernice. *Sidney Rella and the Glass Sneaker.* Illus. by the author. Macmillan, 1985. (ISBN 0-02-767790-7; unp.; Grades 1–3)

Left behind to do the chores when his older brothers head off for football practice, Sidney wishes he could make the team. The arrival of a wand-toting fairy godfather makes it come true.

Pollock, Penny. *The Turkey Girl: A Zuni Cinderella Story.* Illus. by Ed Young. Little, Brown, 1996. (ISBN 0-316-71314-7; unp.; Grades 2–5)

A poor outcast girl who faithfully tends her flock of turkeys confides in them her dreams of attending the Dance of the Sacred Bird, and they provide her with clothes and a warning to return before sunset. This is a dark and provocative Cinderella variant, with an ending listeners will be eager to discuss.

Vande Velde, Vivian. *A Hidden Magic.* Illus. by Trina Schart Hyman. Crown, 1985. (ISBN 0-517-55534-4; 117p.; Grades 3–6)

Jennifer, a plain, shy, kind princess, travels into the enchanted forest with visiting Prince Alexander, vain and self-important, and sets out to find a way to undo a sleeping spell the Prince brings upon himself.

Wilsdorf, Anne. *Princess*. Illus. by the author. Greenwillow, 1993. (ISBN 0-688-11542-X; unp.; Grades K–3)

In a cute take-off on Andersen's "The Princess and the Pea," Prince Leopold's mother reminds him that only a certified-genuine princess is worthy of him, though he can't find a suitable mate until he meets a shepherdess named Princess.

Yolen, Jane. *Sleeping Ugly*. Illus. by Diane Stanley. Coward, 1981. (ISBN 0-698-20617-7; unp.; Grades 2–4)

Of two girls—beautiful but nasty Princess Miserella and kind orphan Plain Jane—it's the latter whose personality wins her three wishes from a fairy-in-disguise.

Go Get the Axe

Grade Level: 3–6

Peeping through the knothole of grampa's wooden leg,
Who'll wind the clock when I am gone?
Go get the axe, there's a flea in Lizzie's ear,
And a boy's best friend is his mother.

Peeping through the knothole of grampa's wooden leg,
Why do they build the shore so near the ocean?
Who cut the sleeves out of dear old Daddy's vest
And dug up Fido's bones to build the sewer?

A horsey stood around with his feet on the ground.
Who'll wind the clock when I am gone?
Go get the axe, there's a fly in Lizzie's ear,
But a boy's best friend is his mother.

I fell from a window, a second-story window;
I caught my eyebrow on the windowsill.
The cellar's behind the door, Mary's room's behind the axe,
But a boy's best friend is his mother.

Go Get the Axe

From Carl Sandburg's *The American Songbag*. Harcourt, 1927.

Peep - ing through the knot-hole of gram - pa's wood - en

leg,_____ Who'll wind the clock when I am

gone?_____ Go get the

axe, there's a flea in Liz - zie's ear, And a

boy's_____ best friend is his moth - er._____

IN CARL SANDBURG'S *THE AMERICAN SONGBAG*, HE DESCRIBES a "bob-haired blond girl with a dirty face" standing on a Chicago street corner, holding out a tin cup to passersby, singing this merry nonsense song, which apparently was popular in the 1920s. Your students will need you to initiate a discussion about what a knothole is, about clocks that wind and don't have plugs or batteries, and how some songs make no particular sense, which is what makes them funny. I can't figure out what this song means, exactly, but it's always tickled my fancy.

I called my parents to sing the song to them and ask if they had ever heard it as children or had any clue as to what it meant. My father was convinced it referred to Lizzie Borden and the famous case of the 1890s in which she was accused of murdering her parents. My mother didn't know, though she heartily agreed with the line: "But a boy's best friend is his mother." "You've got that right," she said each time I sang it.

Help! Murder! Police!

Chant; Traditional
Grade Level: 2–6

Help! Murder! Police!
My mother fell in the grease.
I laughed so hard, I fell in the lard.
Help! Murder! Police!

FIFTH-GRADE TEACHER CAROL SHIELDS RECITED THIS chant to me some years back, when I was exhorting my students to ransack the memories of their parents and relatives for family chants so we could compile them into a classroom or family collection. The chant is from her hometown of Lowell, Massachusetts, and she was surprised to find herself remembering it after all those years.

"What's lard?" one student asked. Whoops. That meant I forgot a cardinal literary rule: Never take your children's knowledge base for granted. If you think they might not understand a word or phrase, they probably don't, so try to work that vocabulary into your introductory spiel.

Sometimes the chants and songs kids recall aren't exactly suitable for classroom use. I remember singing this jingle, based on a popular commercial in the early 1960s:

I love Bosco; Bosco's good for me;
Mommy put it in my milk to try to poison me.
I fooled Mommy; I put it in her tea.
Now there's no more Mommy to try and poison me.

Your children may have their own stores of "forbidden" lyrics that they may or may not choose to share with you.

Ladies and Jellybeans

Chant; Traditional
Grade Level: 1–6

Ladies and jellybeans, reptiles and crocodiles;

I stand before you to sit behind you

To tell you something I know nothing about.

There's a meeting this evening, just before breakfast

To decide what color to whitewash the church.

There's no admission, just pay at the door;

There's plenty of seats, so just sit on the floor.

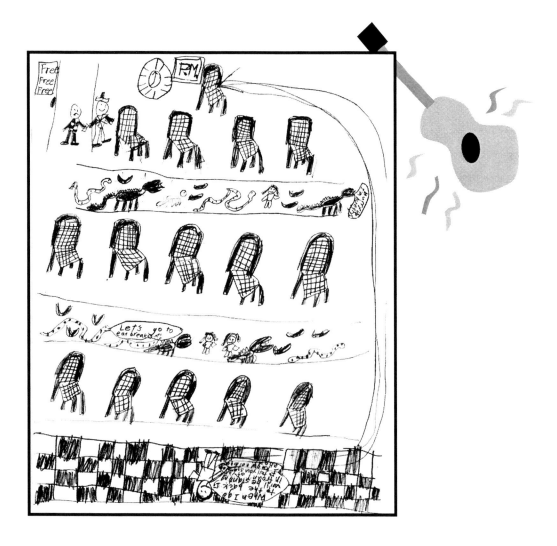

One Bright Day

Traditional
Grade Level: 1–6

One bright day in the middle of the night,

Two dead men got up to fight.

Back to back, they faced each other,

Drew their swords and shot each other.

A deaf policeman heard the noise;

He came and killed those two dead boys.

If you don't believe this lie is true,

Ask the blind man;

He saw it, too.

THE FIRST TIME YOU RECITE "LADIES AND JELLYBEANS," THE boys will say, indignantly, "Jellybeans!" If you change it to "Ladles and Jellybeans," they are much mollified to hear you give the girls an equally ridiculous moniker.

Just for fun, Linda Forte has her fourth graders memorize these two chants on the first day of school every year, telling them they can't go home until they can recite each one. They're stellar examples of nonsense, and I am grateful to the late author and compiler Alvin Schwartz of Princeton, New Jersey, for making so many wonderfully foolish chants and rhymes like these available to our children. Developing a sense of humor, irony, and wordplay is what allows children to comprehend the intricacies of daily life, and Alvin Schwartz certainly made a priceless contribution.

Watch the look of disbelief on your students' faces when you recite the verses with a straight face. Do it several times until it sinks in. Then have them write their own incongruous, paradoxical statements to read aloud.

My Tall Silk Hat

Grade Level: 2–6

One day, as I was riding on the subway,
My tall silk hat, my tall silk hat;

I placed it down upon the seat beside me,
My tall silk hat, my tall silk hat;

A big-a fat-a lady sat upon it,
My tall silk hat, my tall silk hat;

A big-a fat-a lady sat upon it,
(falsetto) My tall silk hat, she squashed it flat.

Christopher Columbus, what do you think of that?
A big-a fat-a lady sat upon my hat.
She was so fat, she squashed my hat,
She was so fat, she squashed my hat,
Christopher Columbus, what do you think of that? HEY!

I REMEMBER SINGING THE ORIGINAL "FUNNICULI, FUNNICULA" in my elementary school chorus, so the parody is all the more amusing for me. Most students these days don't know the real song, which takes away from the humor a bit, but they adore singing this one, ending up with a lusty, shouted "HEY!"

See if you can rustle up a tall black stovepipe-type hat. The collapsible kind would be the best, but the last time I priced one at a flea market, it was $50, a bit steep for a prop.

It's always valuable to have a prop with a song or story, because it focuses children's attention and readies them for the unexpected. I often bring out props and related books stored in unusual and mysterious-looking boxes, and children know there's always a chance of something magical happening during library time.

My Tall Silk Hat

To the tune of "Funniculi, Funnicula"

Hi Ho Librario!

Children's Books to Use with "My Tall Silk Hat"

SEE ALSO BOOKS LISTED UNDER "AIN'T WE CRAZY?" PAGE 89.

Barracca, Debra, and Sal Barracca. *The Adventures of Taxi Dog.* Illus. by Mark Buehner. Dial, 1990. (ISBN 0-8037-0672-3; unp.; Grades K–2)

In an affectionate New York City Checker cab tribute, narrated by dog Maxi, we learn how he went from hungry stray to beloved companion of driver Jim, with whom he rides the Big Apple streets daily.

Brenner, Martha. *Abe Lincoln's Hat.* Illus. by Donald Cook. Random House, 1994. (ISBN 0-679-94977-1; 48p.; Grades 1–4)

That Lincoln used his tall, black hat to store his letters and papers is but one of an

entertaining series of interesting, easy-to-read anecdotes about his life.

Christelow, Eileen. *Olive and the Magic Hat.* Illus. by the author. Clarion, 1987. (ISBN 0-89919-513-X; unp.; Grades K–2)

By accident, Olive Opossum and her little brother Otis knock their father's birthday present, a tall, black hat, out of the window and onto the head of Mr. Foxley, a fox.

Geringer, Laura. *A Three Hat Day.* Illus. by Arnold Lobel. Harper & Row, 1985. (ISBN 0-06-021989-0; unp.; Grades PreK–2)

Hat-lover R. R. Pottle the Third meets Isabel, the woman of his dreams, when he stops in the largest hat store in town to try on a few. Bring in a selection of hats as story props.

Schneider, Howie. *Uncle Lester's Hat*. Illus. by the author. Putnam, 1993. (ISBN 0-399-22439-4; unp.; Grades K–2)

Couch potato Uncle Wilfred takes his hat out for some air and, when a gust blows it away, spends the rest of the book chasing it eastward around the world via boat, goat, camel, and helicopter.

Seuss, Dr. *The 500 Hats of Bartholomew Cubbins*. Illus. by the author. Vanguard, 1938. (ISBN 0-8149-0388-6; unp.; Grades 1–3)

King Derwin of Didd is furious when young Bartholomew can't seem to take his hat off his head without another one appearing there in its place, and he orders the boy arrested and beheaded.

Smath, Jerry. *A Hat So Simple*. Illus. by the author. BridgeWater, 1993. (ISBN 0-8167-3016-4; unp.; Grades PreK–2)

Though all alligator Edna wants is a small and neat little hat to keep her cool while fishing with her husband, instead she takes the advice of friends and buys a bigger hat that causes her nothing but trouble.

Smith, William Jay. *Ho for a Hat!* Illus. by Lynn Munsinger. Little, Brown, 1989. (ISBN 0-316-80120-8; unp.; Grades PreK–2)

What's the reason for hats? "They look nice/ They feel nice/ They *are* nice." Expect everyone to holler the chantable title refrain. Declare Inventive Hat Day, when children create and wear outrageous hats with found materials and have a Hat Parade.

Weiss, Nicki, sel. *If You're Happy and You Know It: Eighteen Story Songs Set to Pictures*. Illus. by the author. Greenwillow, 1987. (ISBN 0-688-06444-2; 40p.; Grades PreK–2)

You'll find a nice version of "My Tall Silk Hat" in this attractive songbook that children can read themselves.

I Wish I Was a Honosaurarius

Grade Level: 2–6

I wish I was a honosaurarius, a repopotanomy, ha ha ha ha.

But since I'm not, and never can hope to be

A honosaurarius, a repopotanomy,

I'm a June bug, I'm an egghead,

And I went and bashed my head against the wall—

Boom! ha ha ha ha.

I wish I was a honosaurarius, a repopotanomy, ha ha ha ha.

But since I'm not, and never can hope to be

A honosaurarius, a repopotanomy,

I'm a moonball, I'm a teabag,

And I often hit my head against my rear—

Kaboom! ha ha ha ha.

I Wish I Was a Honosaurarius

Camp song

wall.———— Boom!   ha   ha   ha   ha.

NQUIRING MINDS WILL WANT TO KNOW: WHAT'S A HONOSAUR-
arius? How about a repopotanomy? Beats me. I don't know what a moonball is,
either. So why not ask the kids to draw each one. There is no social significance to
this song as far as I am aware, but it's satisfying to sing after a long, hard day in the
classroom when everyone is going bonkers anyway.

SEE BOOKS LISTED UNDER "AIN'T WE CRAZY?" PAGE 89.

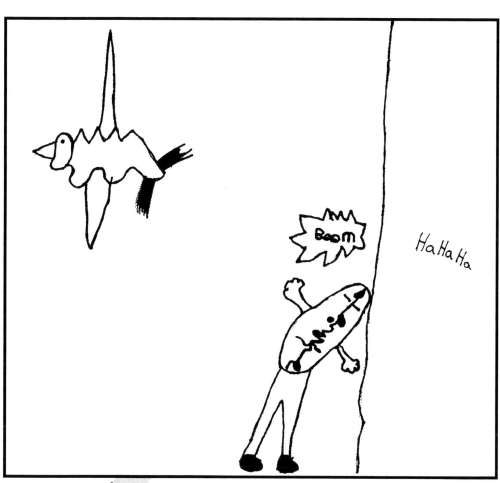

Trolley Song

Grade Level: 2–6

Ding, ding, ding, ding, ding,

There goes my trolley, my kiddycar, my bus

To take me to the nutty factory;

Just like the nuts that fall, I'm a little cracked that's all,

Ding, ding, ding, ding, ding,

There goes my trolley, my kiddycar, my bus.

When we sing this thoroughly dumb song, we like to pretend to pull a bell cord for each "ding."

SEE BOOKS LISTED UNDER "AIN'T WE CRAZY?" PAGE 89.

Trolley Song

Camp song

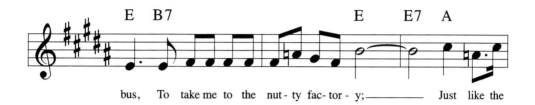

Ding, ding, ding, ding, ding, There goes my trol-ley, my kid-dy car, my

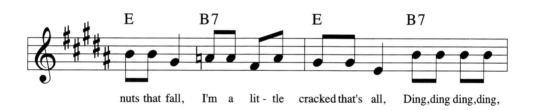

bus, To take me to the nut-ty fac-tor-y;————— Just like the

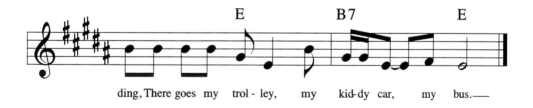

nuts that fall, I'm a lit-tle cracked that's all, Ding, ding ding, ding,

ding, There goes my trol-ley, my kid-dy car, my bus.——

My Father Shot a Kangaroo

Grade Level: 2–6

My father shot a kangaroo,

And he gave me the gristly part to chew;

Now wasn't that a horrible thing to do?

To give me to chew the gristly part of a dead kangaroo!

PAM SWALLOW, CHILDREN'S BOOK AUTHOR AND FRIEND TO all animals, is squeamish about this song and winces when I mention it. She's taking it too literally, of course. In Australia, where people do eat kangaroo meat, this song may be taken as fact, perhaps; but in the United States, kids find the idea of eating kangaroos comical, as absurd as eating elephants.

I learned all three of the preceding songs at Camp Dark Waters in Medford, New Jersey, in 1960, when I was eight. I learned many things at camp during that and many subsequent summers, but the songs, as mindless as they are, have stayed with me forever.

My Father Shot a Kangaroo

Camp song

My fa - ther shot a kan-ga-roo, And he gave me the gri-s-tly part to chew; Now was-n't that a hor-ri-ble thing to do? To give me to chew the gri-s-tly part of a dead kan-ga-roo!

In 1995 I went back to Camp Dark Waters for a Labor Day weekend reunion and spent time with people I hadn't seen in 30 years. They gave out copies of the camp songbooks, which had been typed on an old typewriter and run off on dittoes decades before. I was astonished at how many of the songs I remembered, but especially by how many of them I still sing with my students.

Girl and Boy Scouts are still learning witty new songs every year, and if you ask older children to fill you in on what's hot to sing in the scouting community, you'll get a valuable earful. Tape record the children singing these songs so you have it on hand later, when you can't remember the tunes.

SEE BOOKS LISTED UNDER "AIN'T WE CRAZY?" PAGE 89.

I Sat Next to the Duchess at Tea

Grade Level: 2–6

I sat next to the duchess at tea.

It was just as I thought it would be;

Her rumblings abdominal were simply phenomenal,

And everyone thought it was me!

I Sat Next to the Duchess at Tea

By Pat Shaw

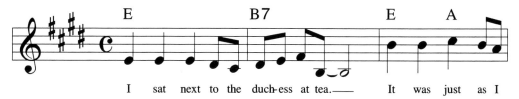

I sat next to the duch-ess at tea.—— It was just as I

thought it would be.—— Her rum - bl - ings ab - dom - in - al were

sim - p - ly phe-nom - e - nal, And ev-ery-one thought it was me!

YOU'LL NEED TO GO OVER THE VOCABULARY IN THIS delightful little number so children can absorb the humor. "Oh, you mean her stomach was growling! Now I get it!" will be a typical response.

Kids like saying that third line over and over. It's so rhythmic and catchy. Make sure to draw out the words "rumblings" and "simply" to "rum-bel-lings" and "sim-pel-ly" so they roll off your tongue.

This can be done as a round, of course, so once your listeners know it by heart, try it in two or four parts, depending on your stamina.

SEE BOOKS LISTED UNDER "AIN'T WE CRAZY?" PAGE 89.

Oh I Had a Little Chicken / I Went to Cincinnati

Grade Level: K–6

Oh I had a little chicken, and she couldn't lay an egg,

So I poured hot water up and down her leg,

And the little chicken cried, and the little chicken begged,

And the little chicken laid a hard-boiled egg.

Oh I went to Cincinnati, and I walked around the block,

And I walked right into a bakery shop,

And I picked two doughnuts out of the grease,

And I handed the lady a five-cent piece.

Well, she looked at the nickel, and she looked at me,

She said, "This nickel's no good to me;

There's a hole in the middle, and it's all the way through."

Said I, "There's a hole in the doughnut, too.

Thanks for the doughnut. Goodbye."

YOU DON'T NEED A REASON TO SING THIS OR ANY OTHER NON-sense song, but there's something so satisfyingly simple about this one's logic that it fits in perfectly with some of the dizzier chicken stories listed below. I have a large, white plastic egg that I pull out when I sing this, and then I pretend to crack it on someone's head.

With second or third graders, ask them if they remember the time Ramona cracked a raw egg on her head in *Ramona Quimby, Age 8* by Beverly Cleary (Morrow, 1981), and laugh and wince over that embarrassing lunchroom incident. Or with fourth or fifth graders, recall the time Homer Price's uncle's doughnut machine wouldn't stop cranking out thousands of doughnuts, even though they pulled the plug, in *Homer Price* by Robert McCloskey (Viking, 1943).

Sometimes the songs will trigger memories of another book or a poem or a joke. That's one thing I love about teaching in the library. Whenever an unexpected book springs to mind, I can whip it off the shelf, give an instant booktalk to my students, and hand the book out to an eager reader.

Oh I Had a Little Chicken / I Went to Cincinnati

To the tune of "Turkey in the Straw"   Traditional

I like to start a lesson with a story, a poem, a song, a riddle, an anecdote, or a stumper. I collect stumper stories for which children must figure out the correct answer. Here's one I loved as a child. It still stymies kids:

A rooster flew to the top of a barn roof. It was a red roof and it was steeply slanted on both sides.When the bird laid an egg, which way did it roll—to the right or to the left?

Children will have several answers for this story, until one finally pipes up with the correct one: "Neither. Roosters don't lay eggs!"

Children's Books to Use with "Oh I Had a Little Chicken"

See also books listed under "Ain't We Crazy?" page 89.

Andersen, Hans Christian. *It's Perfectly True*. Adapted and illus. by Janet Stevens. Holiday House, 1988. (ISBN 0-8234-0672-5; unp.; Grades 1–6)

A jolly hen's words, made in jest, are repeated by a gossip in the henhouse, and as the story is passed along, it is changed, exaggerated, and improved upon, showing how "one little feather can become five dead hens." Play the game "Telephone," also known as "Whisper down the Lane," to demonstrate how stories can evolve.

Auch, Mary Jane. *The Easter Egg Farm*. Illus. by the author. Holiday House, 1992. (ISBN 0-8234-0917-1; unp.; Grades K–2)

At first, hen Pauline is afraid of the different-looking eggs that she lays, but human Mrs. Pennywort, deducing that each wonderful egg resembles whatever Pauline sees as she is laying it, comes up with new and creative scenarios to inspire her hen. Children can draw pictures of eggs they'd like to see Pauline lay.

Auch, Mary Jane. *Eggs Mark the Spot*. Illus. by the author. Holiday House, 1996. (ISBN 0-8234-1242-3; unp.; Grades K–3)

Talented hen Pauline, who lays eggs with images on each shell of what she sees around her, is invited to the Big City Art Gallery to lay an egg inspired by each famous painting on display. If you get into identifying each artist represented, you'll also get a charge out of Thatcher Hurd's *Art Dog* (HarperCollins, 1996).

Auch, Mary Jane. *Peeping Beauty*. Illus. by the author. Holiday House, 1993. (ISBN 0-8234-1001-3; unp.; Grades K–3)

Planning to become a famous ballet dancer someday, hen Pauline allows herself to be taken in by a fox who promises to make her a star.

Ernst, Lisa Campbell. *Zinnia and Dot*. Illus. by the author. Viking, 1992. (ISBN 0-670-83091-7; unp.; Grades K–2)

Two fat, vain, competitive chickens, left with a single egg between them after a crafty weasel steals the rest, compete over the egg-sitting until they are faced with a threat to their unhatched chick.

Heine, Helme. *The Most Wonderful Egg in the World*. Illus. by the author. Atheneum, 1983. (ISBN 0-689-50280-X; unp.; Grades PreK–2)

Three hens, quarreling about which is the most beautiful, seek advice from the king, who tells them he will make a princess of the one who lays the most wonderful egg.

Kellogg, Steven. *Chicken Little*. Illus. by the author. Morrow, 1985. (ISBN 0-688-05691-1; unp.; Grades K–2)

In a slapstick modernized version of the old folktale, Foxy Loxy impersonates a police officer, but Chicken Little prevails anyway.

King-Smith, Dick. *Pretty Polly*. Illus. by Marshall Peck. Crown, 1992. (ISBN 0-517-58606-1; 120p.; Grades 2–4)

Farm girl Abigail can't afford to buy an expensive talking parrot, so she decides instead to train a baby chick to talk.

Marshall, James. *Wings: A Tale of Two Chickens*. Illus. by the author. Viking, 1986. (ISBN 0-670-80961-6; unp.; Grades K–2)

Bored chicken Winnie, who hasn't a lick of sense because she never reads, is taken in by a smooth-talking fox when he invites her aboard his hot-air balloon.

Pinkwater, Daniel. *The Hoboken Chicken Emergency*. Illus. by the author. Simon & Schuster, 1990. (ISBN 0-671-73980-8; 83p.; Grades 3–5)

Arthur brings home a six-foot, 266-pound live chicken for Thanksgiving, planning to keep it for a pet, but it escapes, terrorizing the good citizens of Hoboken, New Jersey. "Mama, it's a very big chicken!" is one of my favorite memorable lines in children's books.

Ain't We Crazy?

Grade Level: 2–6

Oh I have a little ditty, it's as crazy as can be;

The guy that wrote it said he wanted it and handed it to me.

But I found I couldn't use it, just because it sounded blue,

And that's the very reason why I'm handing it to you.

It's a song the alligators sing while coming though the rye,

As they serenade the elephants up in the trees so high.

The iceman hums this ditty as he shovels in the coal,

And the monkeys join the chorus up around the northern pole.

CHORUS:

> Ain't we crazy? Ain't we crazy?
>
> This is the way we pass the time away.
>
> Ain't we crazy? Ain't we crazy?
>
> We're going to sing this song all night today.

It was midnight on the ocean, not a streetcar was in sight,

And the sun was shining brightly, for it rained all day that night;

'Twas a summer night in winter and the rain was snowing fast,

And a barefoot boy with shoes on stood a-sitting in the grass.

It was evening, and the rising sun was setting in the west,

And the little fishes in the trees were huddled in their nests;

The rain was pouring down, and the moon was shining bright,

And everything that you could see was hidden out of sight.
CHORUS

While the cows were making cowslips, and the bells were wringing wet,

And the bumblebees were making bums and smoking cigarettes,

A man slept in a stable and came out a little hoarse,

So he hopped upon his golf sticks and drove all around the course.

"Good evening, sir," a woman said, and her eyes were bright with tears,
As she put her head beneath her feet and stood that way for years.
Her children six were orphans, all except one tiny tot
Who lives in the house across the street upon the vacant lot.
CHORUS

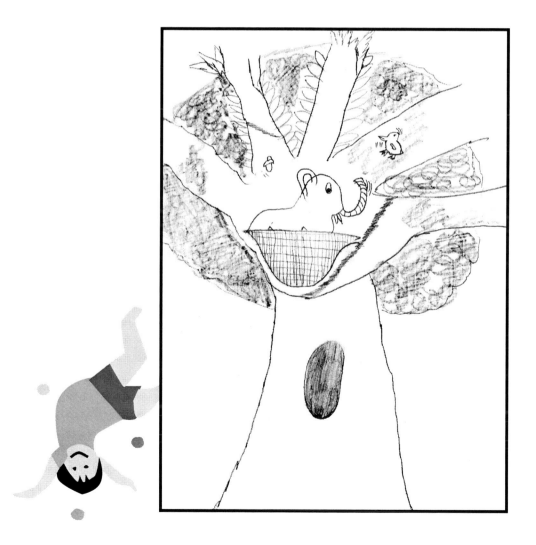

Ain't We Crazy?

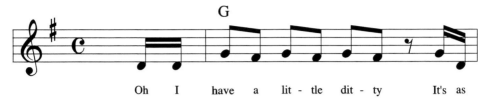

Oh I have a lit - tle dit - ty It's as

cra - zy as can be; The guy that wrote it said he want - ed it and

hand - ed it to me.— But I found I could - n't use it, just be -

cause it sound - ed blue, And that's the ve - ry rea - son why I'm

REFRAIN

hand - ing it to you. Ain't we cra - zy? Ain't we

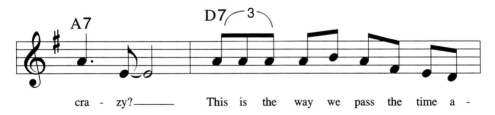

cra - zy?——— This is the way we pass the time a -

way.——— Ain't we cra - zy? Ain't we cra - zy? We're

go - ing to sing this song all night to - day.

AS IN "ONE BRIGHT DAY" AND "LADIES AND JELLYBEANS," this song is crammed with incongruities or paradoxes that children delight in pointing out. Upon first hearing it, some will get indignant, "How could it be a summer night in winter? This song doesn't make sense!"

On the second go-round, with words in hand, children will begin to pick out examples of just how crazy the song is and will realize that it's that way on purpose. This is a prime song to have children illustrate, as that allows them to visualize each wacky image and then share it with the rest of the group.

Children's Books to Use with "Ain't We Crazy?"

Booth, David, comp. *Doctor Knickerbocker and Other Rhymes.* Illus. by Maryann Kovalski. Ticknor & Fields, 1993. (ISBN 0-395-67168-X; 72p.; Grades 2–5)

There are scores of children's school yard rhymes here, both recent and from the past, accompanied by droll, detailed, Victorian-flavored pen-and-ink drawings.

Brewton, Sara, John E. Brewton, and G. Meredith Blackburn III, comps. *My Tang's Tungled and Other Ridiculous Situations.* Illus. by Graham Booth.Crowell, 1973. (ISBN 0-690-57223-9; 111p.; Grades 2–6)

The more than 100 funny poems and bits of nonsense, including limericks and tongue twisterish verse, are ripe for memorizing.

Cole, Joanna, and Stephanie Calmenson. *Six Sick Sheep: 101 Tongue Twisters.* Illus. by Alan Tiegreen. Morrow, 1993. (ISBN 0-688-11140-8; 64p.; Grades 1–5)

Amusing black pen-and-inks accompany the many tongue twisters, which are arranged by broad subject and stretch from single phrases to whole poems.

Cole, William, comp. *Oh, Such Foolishness!* Illus. by Tomie dePaola. HarperCollins, 1991. (ISBN 0-397-32502-9; 96p.; Grades 2–6)

You'll find plenty of read-aloud laughs in this genial collection of 58 nonsense poems.

Emrich, Duncan, comp. *The Hodgepodge Book.* Illus. by Ib Ohlsson. Four Winds, 1972. (ISBN 0-590-07250-1; 367p.; Grades 2–6)

Along with Emrich's *The Nonsense Book* (1970) and *The Whim-Wham Book* (1975), this is an essential compilation of American folklore, containing riddles, jokes, puzzles, and "all manner of curious, interesting, and out-of-the way information."

Legge, David. *Bamboozled.* Illus. by the author. Scholastic, 1995. (ISBN 0-590-47989-X; unp.; Grades K–2)

A girl describes an ordinary visit with Grandpa at his house, though the pictures are overrun with surreal, bizarre, and outlandish incongruities that children will pore over. They'll enjoy drawing pictures of redesigned, *Bamboozled*-style rooms from their own houses.

Levitt, Paul M., Douglas A. Burger, and Elissa S. Guralnick. *The Weighty Word Book.* Illus. by Janet Stevens. Manuscripts Ltd., 1990. (ISBN 0-9627979-0-1; 100p.; Grades 4–8)

The pun-laden short stories in this genial, creative, and instructive alphabetical collection teach the meanings of 26 difficult words—*abasement, bifurcate, coruscate, dogmatic*, and then some—so you'll never forget them. Use the story about the Parrot Ox to introduce what a paradox is when you sing "Ain't We Crazy?" or recite "One Bright Day" and "Ladies and Jellybeans."

Most, Bernard. *Zoodles.* Illus. by the author. Harcourt, 1992. (ISBN 0-15-299969-8; unp.; Grades 1–4)

"What do you call a kangaroo that wakes you up every day? A kangarooster!" The 15 riddles, each about two animals with linking names, will spur children to make up their own.

Opie, Iona, and Peter Opie, eds. *I Saw Esau: The Schoolchild's Pocket Book.* Illus. by Maurice Sendak. Candlewick, 1992. (ISBN 1-56402-046-0; 160p.; Grades 1–5)

This small-sized gem of a collection, first published in 1946, contains many satisfying chants, rhymes, riddles, tongue twisters, and insults that children say to each other when they think there are no grown-ups about.

Phillips, Louis. *263 Brain Busters: Just How Smart Are You, Anyway?* Illus. by James Stevenson. Viking Kestrel, 1985. (ISBN 0-670-80412-6; 87p.; Grades 3–6)

Math problems, verbal tricks, story problems, and other clever stumpers will get your students thinking, arguing, and reasoning.

Prelutsky, Jack, comp. *Poems of A. Nonny Mouse.* Illus. by Henrik Drescher. Knopf, 1989. (ISBN 0-394-98711-X; unp.; Grades K–4)

In his introduction, Prelutsky explains that all those nutty nonsense poems erroneously attributed to "Anonymous" were actually penned by A. Nonny Mouse and records 70 of them here. *A. Nonny Mouse Writes Again* (1993) is the companion volume.

Raffi. *Down by the Bay.* Illus. by Nadine Bernard Westcott. Crown, 1987 (ISBN 0-517-56644-3; unp.; Grades K–2)

"Did you ever see a fly wearing a tie?" Children love to make up new verses to this cheerfully silly song.

Rosen, Michael, sel. *Walking the Bridge of Your Nose.* Illus. by Chloë Cheese. Kingfisher, 1995. (ISBN 1-85697-596-7; 61p.; Grades 1–5)

You will pore over this delightful collection of wordplay and poems, including variants of "Ain't We Crazy?" and "Ladies and Jellybeans" and wacky versions of common nursery rhymes.

Schwartz, Alvin, comp. *And the Green Grass Grew All Around: Folk Poetry from Everyone.* Illus. by Sue Truesdale. HarperCollins, 1992. (ISBN 0-06-022758-3; 195p.; Grades 2–6)

A singable, chantable, and affable anthology of more than 300 poems, riddles, songs, and chants, collected from kids everywhere.

Schwartz, Alvin, comp. *I Saw You in the Bathtub and Other Folk Rhymes.* Illus. by Syd Hoff. Harper & Row, 1989. (ISBN 0-06-025298-7; 64p.; Grades K–3)

The three dozen easy-to-read chants and poems in this simple collection will be devoured by eager readers.

Schwartz, Alvin, comp. *Tomfoolery: Trickery and Foolery with Words.* Illus. by Glen Rounds. Lippincott, 1973. (ISBN 0-397-31466-3; 127p.; Grades 1–6)

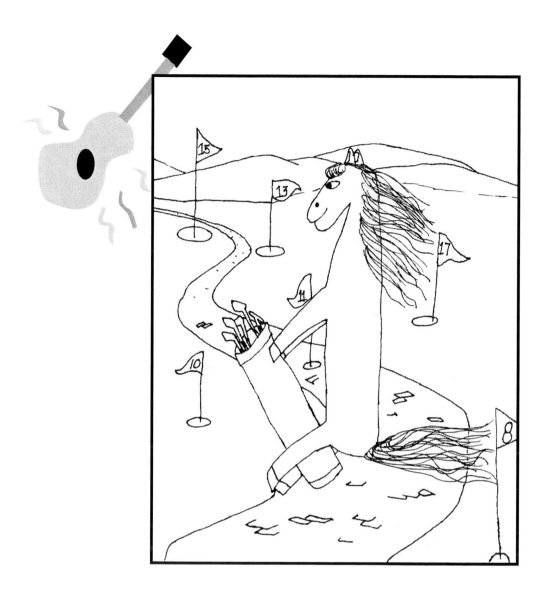

One of my favorite books of jokes, riddles, tricks, and just plain foolishness, this collection includes "Ladies and Jellybeans" and "One Bright Day."

Schwartz, Alvin. *A Twister of Twists, a Tangler of Tongues.* Illus. by Glen Rounds. HarperCollins, 1972. (ISBN 0-06-446004-5; 128p.; Grades 2–6)

Arranged by subject, this thorough compilation of tongue twisters even includes a section in nine foreign languages.

Steig, William. *CDB.* Illus. by the author. Simon & Schuster, 1987. (ISBN 0-671-66689-4; unp.; Grades 2–6)

On each page there is a pen-and-ink drawing with a caption made up of letters that, when spoken, form a real sentence. CDB translates into "see the bee." Write each set of letters on the board for kids to figure out, and then fool around with the alphabet to write and illustrate new coded sentences.

Terban, Marvin. *Funny You Should Ask: How to Make Up Jokes and Riddles with Wordplay.* Illus. by John O'Brien. Clarion, 1992. (ISBN 0-395-60556-3; 64p.; Grades 3–6)

A step-by-step explanation of how wordplay works, this takes us through jokes with homonyms, homographs, and idioms and gets us started composing new ones.

Tripp, Wallace, comp. *A Great Big Ugly Man Came Up and Tied His Horse to Me; A Book of Nonsense Verse*. Illus. by the author. Little, Brown, 1973. (ISBN 0-316-85280-5; 46p.; Grades K–3)

There are about three dozen bits of pleasingly silly verse here, accompanied by endearing and expressive animals rendered in pen and ink and watercolor.

Withers, Carl, comp. *A Rocket in My Pocket: The Rhymes and Chants of Young Americans*. Illus. by Susanne Suba. Holt, 1948. (ISBN 0-8050-0821-7; 214p.; Grades K–4)

Search your memory to see if you recall these classic jump-rope, bounce-ball, autograph-album, or counting-out rhymes.

Wood, Audrey. *Bright and Early Thursday Evening: A Tangled Tale*. Illus. by Don Wood. Harcourt, 1996. (ISBN 0-15-200363-0; unp.; Grades K–4)

Adorned with huge, bright, surreal digital art, this incongruous picture book poem careens through a lie-filled day with the curly-maned narrator waking up and dreaming she is dead, dressing up for her funeral, and marrying a potato dressed in gabardine pants.

Chapter 3

Alligator Pie

Playing with Your Food

PRESCHOOL TEACHER CHERYL GERARD BRINGS HER TWO classes of special-needs children to the library for stories and songs every week. The morning group of just-three-year-olds is mostly nonverbal, while the more worldly wise four-year-olds in the afternoon class will respond to questions, laugh at the funny parts in stories, and act out songs and fingerplays.

Each week I scour my shelves for the stories, songs, and fingerplays that will prod the youngest children to open up. They enjoy their library times, it's clear, but to get them to say a word is a challenge. There is one hook that works every time: Talk food.

"How many of you love pizza?"

"I love pizza," a child invariably blurts out.

"With mushrooms?" I ask.

"Noooo!" they'll cry in horror.

"How about pepperoni?"

"Yes, pepperoni," comes the reply.

Ask them who likes spaghetti or ice cream or cookies, and all of a sudden the formerly taciturn pipe up. Reading stories with food is a vicarious thrill. Food does that to us all. Just the mention of pie makes our mouths water.

Older children love to talk food too. Ask them to name or write about their favorite comfort foods, those treats that make them feel contented and cosseted, from macaroni-and-cheese to chocolate chips.

Just for the sake of diversity and a bit of wickedness, I also like to sing songs with a bit more bite than taste. The following selections have a touch of the macabre and are entertainingly skewed. Children eat them up. You might want to bring in special treats to share when you serve up these tunes.

Alligator Pie

Grade Level: K–6

Alligator pie, alligator pie,
If I don't get some, I think I'm gonna die.
Give away the green grass, give away the sky,
But don't give away my alligator pie.

Alligator stew, alligator stew,
If I don't get some, I don't know what I'll do.
Give away my furry hat, give away my shoe,
But don't give away my alligator stew.

Alligator soup, alligator soup,
If I don't get some, I think I'm gonna droop.
Give away my hockey stick, give away my hoop,
But don't give away my alligator soup.

I FIRST HEARD THIS POEM FROM A RECORD OF CANADIAN POET Dennis Lee reciting his zany, rambunctious verses. It seemed to sing, so I gave it some music.

Children are delighted to find they can write countless new verses for this pattern song. First, brainstorm what other gourmet alligator dishes could be concocted. Over the years, my students have composed on-the-spot verses for Alligator Mousse, Alligator Bread, Alligator Cake, Alligator Split, Alligator Toast, and Alligator Fries, to name just a few.

Next, have them come up with possible rhyming words or phrases. Once the group has settled on the best words, sing the new verse with them. Encourage them to jot down additional verses as they think of them, or have them work in teams to come up with stanzas to sing to the whole class.

I introduce this song as a kickoff to a poetry lesson where we explore rhyming, unrhyming, concrete, humorous, and serious poems. From a large, mysterious "magic box," I pull out a prop that ties in to each poem. Songs like Raffi's "The Corner Grocery Store," "Down by the Bay," and "Spider on the Floor" are also perfect for budding versifiers, as is Jo Ellen Bogart's picture book *Gifts* (Scholastic, 1996), where a girl describes the presents her grandmother brings back from around the world.

Alligator Pie

Words by Dennis Lee, ©1974; Music by Judy Freeman

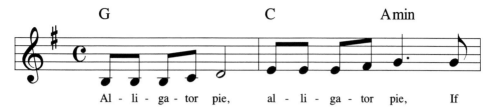

Al - li - ga - tor pie, al - li - ga - tor pie, If

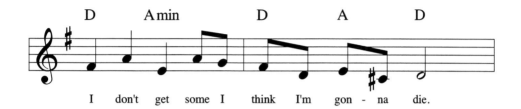

I don't get some I think I'm gon - na die.

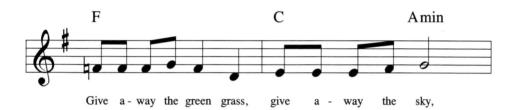

Give a - way the green grass, give a - way the sky,

But don't give a - way my al - li - ga - tor pie.

If we want to make poets and writers out of children, we need to tantalize them with poetry. Read aloud Silverstein, Jack Prelutsky, Barbara Juster Esbensen, Valerie Worth, Judith Viorst, Arnold Adoff, Douglas Florian, Dennis Lee, J. Patrick Lewis, Eve Merriam, Marilyn Singer, and Jane Yolen, just for starters. Read poetry that's serious, comical, somber, ironical, probing, quizzical, descriptive, farcical, free verse, rhythmical, flowery, or cynical. Read it more than once. Kids don't usually "get it" the first time through.

Hearing poetry makes one want to write poetry. Inspiration and writing ideas can come anytime and from everywhere. Make sure pencil and paper are close at hand. If we write down our insightful musings—no matter how far-fetched—right away, they won't evaporate.

Also use this song as an opening to compare fiction and nonfiction books on the subject of crocodiles and to explore the differences between alligators and crocodiles. I have a perfectly tacky alligator purse that I use to introduce the poem "Tiny Tim" ("In came the doctor, in came the nurse, in came the lady with the alligator purse"), which also works well here.

Children's Books to Use with "Alligator Pie"

SEE ALSO FOOD-RELATED BOOKS LISTED UNDER "WHO THREW THE OVERALLS IN MRS. MURPHY'S CHOWDER?" PAGE 104.

Aliki. *Keep Your Mouth Closed, Dear.* Illus. by the author. Dial, 1966. (ISBN 0-8037-4418-8; unp.; Grades PreK–2)

Much to his parents' dismay, every time young crocodile Charles opens his mouth he manages to swallow something large, including a wooden spoon, a clock, and his father's hat.

Bare, Colleen Stanley. *Never Kiss an Alligator!* Photos by the author. Cobblehill/Dutton, 1989. (ISBN 0-525-65003-2; unp.; Grades K–3)

Close-up color photographs and a fascinating fact-filled text provide an overview of alligator life in the southern swamps of the United States.

Cushman, Doug. *Possum Stew.* Illus. by the author. Dutton, 1990. (ISBN 0-525-44566-8; unp.; Grades K–2)

Claiming that he can help them catch Old Catfish, hungry Old Possum tricks both Gator and Bear by tying their fishing lines together and running off with their baskets of fresh-caught fish, but he is tricked in return.

Dahl, Roald. *The Enormous Crocodile.* Illus. by Quentin Blake. Knopf, 1978. (ISBN 0-394-83594-8; unp.; Grades K–3)

Plotting to capture a juicy little child to eat, the Enormous Crocodile is foiled each time by the other animals of the jungle.

Hurd, Thacher. *Mama Don't Allow.* Illus. by the author. Harper & Row, 1984. (ISBN 0-06-022690-0; unp.; Grades K–2)

Saxophonist Miles and three fellow possum musicians form the Swamp Band and play a Saturday night gig at the Alligator Ball until the alligators get hungry for Swamp Band Soup. Music to the title song is appended.

Kipling, Rudyard. *The Elephant's Child.* Illus. by Lorinda Bryan Cauley. Harcourt, 1983. (ISBN 0-15-225385-8; 48p.; Grades 1–4)

In Kipling's famous tale, the Elephant's Child—with a blackish, bulgy nose as big as a boot—asks the Crocodile what he has for dinner and has his nose pulled badly out of shape by the Crocodile in response.

Lee, Dennis. *Alligator Pie.* Illus. by Frank Newfield. Houghton Mifflin, 1974. OP; 64p.; Grades PreK–4)

I finally located a paperback of this wonderful collection of nursery-rhyme-like poems published by Macmillan of Canada. I sure wish Houghton Mifflin in the United States would reprint it!

Mathews, Louise. *Gator Pie.* Illus. by Jeni Bassett. Sundance, 1995. (ISBN 0-7608-0005-7; unp.; Grades K–2)

Alvin and Alice Gator find a huge uncut pie on a table by the swamp and, as other fierce, hungry gators amble up, try to decide what fraction of the pie each should get; from half, to thirds, quarters, eighths, and even hundredths.

Novak, Matt. *Gertie and Gumbo.* Illus. by the author. Orchard, 1995. (ISBN 0-531-08778-6; unp.; Grades K–2)

At Gertie's papa's theater, the Goomba Palace, Papa wrestles five tough alligators in front of spectators. But when one alligator lays an egg, young Gertie raises baby Gumbo to dance and play the piano.

Palatini, Margie. *Piggie Pie.* Illus. by Howard Fine. Clarion, 1995. (ISBN 0-395-71691-8; unp.; Grades K–3)

Distressed over the lack of the key ingredient for her special recipe, Gritch the Witch sets out for Old MacDonald's Farm ("just over the river and through the woods"), where she finds every animal except the piggies she seeks, and instead hooks up with the emaciated but wily wolf, who agrees to come home with her for dinner. Kids can act this one out and write new recipes for Gritch's "Old Hag Cookbook."

Raffi. *Down by the Bay.* Illus. by Nadine Bernard Westcott. Crown, 1987. (ISBN 0-517-56644-3; unp.; Grades PreK–2)

"Did you ever see a fly wearing a tie?" When your children have filled up on Alligator Pie, have them make up new verses to this cheerfully silly song.

Raffi. *Spider on the Floor.* Words and music by Bill Russell. Illus. by True Kelley. Crown, 1993. (ISBN 0-517-59464-1; unp.; Grades PreK–2)

In a rhyming song that incorporates the parts of the body, a big, hairy spider climbs up a lady's leg, stomach, neck, and head before jumping off to start again. This is another easily learned song for which children can think up many new rhyming verses.

Sendak, Maurice. *Alligators All Around.* Illus. by the author. Harper & Row, 1962. (ISBN 0-06-025530-7; unp.; Grades PreK–1)

Take an alligator-led tour of the alphabet, with each letter consisting of two-word alliterative action phrases ("bursting balloons"), perfect for acting out in creative drama.

Westcott, Nadine Bernard. *The Lady with the Alligator Purse.* Illus. by the author. Joy Street/Little, Brown, 1988. (ISBN 0-316-93035-7; unp.; Grades PreK–1)

"Miss Lucy had a baby, / His name was Tiny Tim" is the start of a well-loved chant that children love to memorize. Instead of the tot sliding down the drain, in this version he ends up with pizza. Children can recite this, act it out, and draw their own pizza with inventive toppings.

Who Threw the Overalls in Mrs. Murphy's Chowder?

Grade Level: 2–6

CHORUS:

> Who threw the overalls in Mrs. Murphy's chowder?
>
> Nobody spoke, so we shouted all the louder.
>
> It's an Irish trick, it's true,
>
> And I'll lick the one who threw
>
> The overalls in Mrs. Murphy's chowder.

Mrs. Murphy gave a party 'bout a week ago;

Everything was plentiful, well, the Murphys they're not slow.

They treated us like gentlemen, we tried to act the same;

Only for what happened, it was an awful shame.

Mrs. Murphy dished the chowder out and fainted on the spot;

She'd found a pair of overalls at the bottom of the pot.

Tim Nolan he got ripping mad, his eyes were bulging out;

He jumped upon the piano and loudly he did shout:

CHORUS

They dragged the pants from out the soup and laid 'em on the floor;

Each man swore upon his life he'd not seen 'em before.

They were plastered up with mortar and were worn out at the knee;

They'd had their many ups and downs as we could plainly see.

When Mrs. Murphy she came to, she starts to cry and pout;

She'd had them in the wash that day, forgot to take 'em out.

Tim Nolan he excused himself for what he'd said that night,

So we put music to the words and sung with all our might:

CHORUS

Who Threw the Overalls in Mrs. Murphy's Chowder?

Words and music by George L. Geifer, ©1928

Who threw the ov-er-alls in Mrs.— Mur-phy's chow-der?

No-bod——y spoke, so we shout-ed all the loud-er. It's an

I - rish trick, it's true, And I'll lick the one who threw the

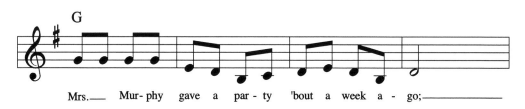

ov - er - alls in Mrs.— Mur-phy's chow———————— der.——————

Mrs.— Mur-phy gave a par-ty 'bout a week a-go;——————

Eve - ry-thing was plen-ti - ful, well, the Mur-phys they're not slow. They

treat - ed us like gen - tle - men, we tried to act the

same;——————— On - ly for what hap - pened, it

was an aw - ful shame.———— Mrs.— Mur - phy dished the

chow - der out and fain - ted on the spot;———— She'd

found a pair of ov - er - alls at the bot - tom of the

pot.———————— Tim No - lan he got

rip - ping mad, his eyes were bul - ging out;———— he jumped up - on the

pi - an - o   and   loud - ly   he   did   shout:

MANY YEARS BACK, FIFTH-GRADE TEACHER CAROL SHIELDS insisted I needed to learn this song to sing with her class on St. Patrick's Day, a holiday she has always celebrated with enthusiasm. "Everyone knows this song," she said incredulously when I told her I had never heard of it, and she dragged me to her house to play her old Bing Crosby record so I could learn it. Ever since, the song has been a staple of the St. Patrick's Day list of songs and stories I tell each year.

It's a mystery, this song, and you'll need to caution children to listen closely to the words to try to figure out the culprit mentioned in the title. Of course, modern children find the idea of using the same pot for laundry and cooking a bit scandalous.

One year, Carol's class and Evelyn Balunis's class made a large pot of chowder and sneaked a pair of miniature Barbie doll overalls into the pot. Mrs. Balunis, dishing out the soup, extracted the pants, exclaiming theatrically, "Who threw the overalls in Mrs. Balunis's chowder?" while the children howled.

You'll want to have a serious discussion of the differences between New England clam chowder (white) and Manhattan clam chowder (red), and perhaps let drop the tidbit that a law on the books in Boston once made it illegal to put tomatoes in clam chowder. Talk about defending your soup turf!

Children's Books to Use with "Who Threw the Overalls in Mrs. Murphy's Chowder?"

Adoff, Arnold. *Chocolate Dreams*. Illus. by Turi MacCombie. Lothrop, 1989. (ISBN 0-688-06823-5; 64p.; Grades 5–8)

Here's a tantalizing batch of free-verse poems about good things to eat, most of which include chocolate.

Adoff, Arnold. *Eats*. Illus. by Susan Russo. Lothrop, 1979. (ISBN 0-688-51901-6; unp.; Grades 2–6)

"Eats are on my mind" starts a delicious collection of more than three dozen free-verse poems about food, from chocolate to popcorn.

Cole, William, comp. *Poem Stew*. Illus. by Karen Weinhaus. HarperCollins, 1981. (ISBN 0-06-440136-7; 84p.; Grades 2–5)

There are 57 truly inspired and funny food poems in this satisfying collection.

Goldstein, Bobbye S., sel. *What's on the Menu?* Illus. by Chris L. Demarest. Viking, 1992. (ISBN 0-670-83031-3; unp.; Grades 1–4)

Twenty-five humorous, easy-to-read food poems take eaters from breakfast through bedtime snacks.

Hopkins, Lee Bennett, comp. *Munching: Poems About Eating*. Illus. by Nelle Davis. Little, Brown, 1985. (ISBN 0-316-37269-2; 46p.; Grades K–3)

Make a meal of the 23 tasty poems in this collection.

Keller, Charles. *Belly Laughs! Food Jokes & Riddles*. Illus. by Ron Fritz. Simon & Schuster, 1990. (ISBN 0-671-70068-5; 32p.; Grades 2–6)

"What's the new drink for frogs? Croak-a-Cola!" And five dozen other jocular word-play riddles about food.

Lillegard, Dee. *Do Not Feed the Table*. Illus. by Keiko Narahashi. Delacorte, 1993. (ISBN 0-385-30516-8; unp.; Grades K–3)

The 30 brief, catchy, simple-to-read poems are not about food, but instead describe the appliances and utensils found in every kitchen.

Powell, Polly. *Just Dessert*. Illus. by the author. Harcourt, 1996. (ISBN 0-15-200383-5; unp.; Grades PreK–2)

Lusting after the last piece of Super Yellow Cake with Fudge Frosting, Patsy sneaks out of bed and braves horrible nighttime creatures before she makes it to the fridge.

Westcott, Nadine Bernard, sel. *Never Take a Pig to Lunch and Other Poems About the Fun of Eating*. Illus. by the author. Orchard, 1994. (ISBN 0-531-06834-X; 64p.; Grades 1–4)

More than 60 poems, with wild, tropical-hued pictures on every oversized page, will satisfy the heartiest appetites.

Mrs. Murphy's Chowder

Grade Level: 2–6

Won't you bring back, won't you bring back
  Mrs. Murphy's chowder?

It was tuneful, every spoonful made you yodel louder.

After dinner Uncle Ben used to fill his fountain pen

From a plate of Mrs. Murphy's chowder.

CHORUS:

      It had ice cream, cold cream, benzene, gasoline,

      Soup greens, string beans, floating all around,

      Sponge cake, beefsteak, mistake, stomachache,

      Cream puffs, earmuffs, many to be found;

      Silk hats, doormats, bed slats, Democrats,

      Cowbells, doorbells, beckon you to dine;

      Meatballs, fish balls, mothballs, cannon balls,

      Come on in, the chowder's fine.

Won't you bring back, won't you bring back
  Mrs. Murphy's chowder?

With each helping, you'll be yelping for a headache powder.

And if they had it where you are, you might find a trolley car

In a plate of Mrs. Murphy's chowder.

CHORUS

Won't you bring back, won't you bring back
  Mrs. Murphy's chowder?

You can pack it, you can stack it, all around the larder.

The plumber died the other day; they embalmed him right away

In a bowl of Mrs. Murphy's chowder.

CHORUS

Mrs. Murphy's Chowder

Vaudeville song/Nonsense song

Won't you bring back, won't you bring back—— Mrs.—— Mur-phy's

chow-der? It was tune-ful, ev-ery spoon-ful—— made you yo-del

loud-er.—— Af-ter din-ner Un-cle Ben used to fill his

foun-tain pen from a plate of Mrs.—— Mur-phy's chow——

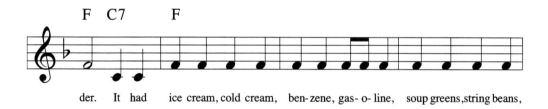

der. It had ice cream, cold cream, ben-zene, gas-o-line, soup greens, string beans,

float-ing all a-round. Sponge cake, beef-steak, mis-take, stomach-ache, cream puffs, ear muffs

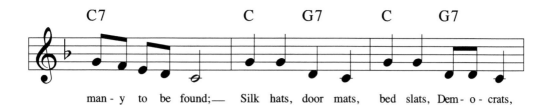

man - y to be found;— Silk hats, door mats, bed slats, Dem - o - crats,

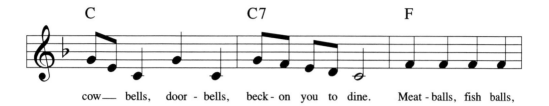

cow— bells, door - bells, beck - on you to dine. Meat - balls, fish balls,

moth - balls, can - non balls, Come on in, the chow - der's fine!

IF THIS IS WHAT MRS. MURPHY PUT INTO HER CHOWDER, it's no wonder she overlooked the overalls! Here's another fun song for children to illustrate. They can also write new recipes for Mrs. Murphy's other tasty dishes, such as bread or pizza or pie.

One of my favorite recipes, for corned beef and cabbage, comes from the kitchen of that notorious Irishwoman Carol Shields. Try this, if you dare:

"Put corned beef, a cabbage, and some potatoes into a pot and cover them with water. Bring it to a boil and cook it for a very long time. When you can't stand the smell anymore, it's done."

SEE FOOD-RELATED BOOKS LISTED UNDER "WHO THREW THE OVERALLS IN MRS. MURPHY'S CHOWDER?" PAGE 104.

In the Boardinghouse

Grade Level: 3–6

In the boardinghouse where I live,
Everything is growing old;
Silver threads are in the butter,
All the bread has turned to mold.

When the dog died, we had hot dogs;
When the cat died, catnip tea;
When the landlord died, I left there;
Spareribs were too much for me.

In the Boardinghouse

To the tune of "Silver Threads Among the Gold"

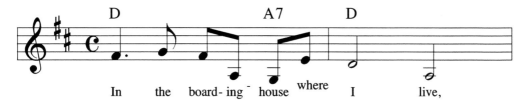

In the board-ing house where I live,

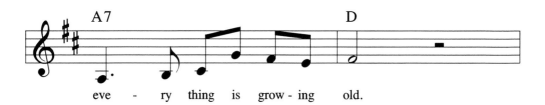

eve - ry thing is grow - ing old.

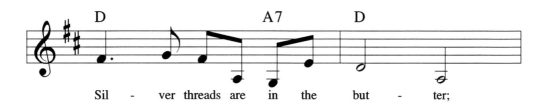

Sil - ver threads are in the but - ter;

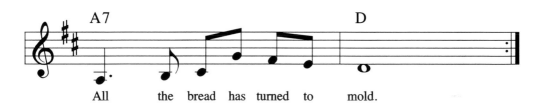

All the bread has turned to mold.

Note: The accompanying recording is in the key of F sharp.

EXPLAIN THAT IT WAS COMMON IN DAYS PAST FOR A SINGLE person to rent a bedroom in a boardinghouse, which provided room and board—meals served in a common dining room with the other boarders. Although the meals may not have been fancy, they were included in the rent. Sing this parody of "Silver Threads Among the Gold" with grave dignity.

SEE FOOD-RELATED BOOKS LISTED UNDER "WHO THREW THE OVERALLS IN MRS. MURPHY'S CHOWDER?" PAGE 104.

Hoimie the Woim

Adapted and retold by Judy Freeman, ©1996
Grade Level: PreK–6

I was sitting on my fence,

Chewing my bubblegum (chomp chomp chomp chomp),

Playing with my yo-yo (doo-wop doo-wop),

When along came HOIMIE THE WOIM.

He was THIS BIG. *(Show with hands 12 inches apart)*

I said, "HOIMIE THE WOIM, what happened?"

He said, "I ATE a RAT!"

I said, "Ohhhh."

And off he went.

I was sitting on my fence,

Chewing my bubblegum (chomp chomp chomp chomp),

Playing with my yo-yo (doo-wop doo-wop),

When along came HOIMIE THE WOIM.

He was THIS BIG. *(Show with hands 18 inches apart)*

I said, "HOIMIE THE WOIM, what happened?"

He said, "I ATE a CAT!"

I said, "Ohhhh."

And off he went.

I was sitting on my fence,

Chewing my bubblegum (chomp chomp chomp chomp),

Playing with my yo-yo (doo-wop doo-wop),

When along came HOIMIE THE WOIM.

He was THIS BIG. *(Show with hands two feet apart)*

I said, "HOIMIE THE WOIM, what happened?"

He said, "I ATE a DOG!"

I said, "Ohhhh."

And off he went.

I was sitting on my fence,

Chewing my bubblegum (chomp chomp chomp chomp),

Playing with my yo-yo (doo-wop doo-wop),

When along came HOIMIE THE WOIM.

He was THIS BIG. *(Show with arms wide apart)*

I said, "HOIMIE THE WOIM, what happened?"

He said, "I ATE a COW!"

I said, "Ohhhh."

And off he went.

I was sitting on my fence,

Chewing my bubblegum (chomp chomp chomp chomp),

Playing with my yo-yo (doo-wop doo-wop),

When along came HOIMIE THE WOIM.

He was THIS BIG. *(Show with finger and thumb, about half an inch apart)*

I said, "HOIMIE THE WOIM, what happened?"

He said, "I *BOIPED*!"

I WAS DRIVING INTO NEW BRUNSWICK ONE DAY WITH A FRIEND, and I wondered if we'd be able to find a parking space.

"Of course we will," she said confidently. "I have parking karma." Sure enough, a space in front of the restaurant emptied and she pulled right in.

"See," she said. "Works every time."

My parking karma is nonexistent, but my book and story karma—finding the right book or story when I need it—works just fine when I concentrate. All librarians and teachers need story karma, and we're all grateful when it kicks in.

Sometimes kismet plays a part too. There I was, sprawled out at the circulation desk in my library late one Friday afternoon, fiddling with the computer, an unwritten speech, and a worm-in-an-apple puppet, when a new first grader, Megan Moskaluk, and her mom wandered in. Of all the libraries in all the towns in New Jersey, Megan walked into mine at just the moment I needed her.

"What are you doing, Miss Freeman?" Megan asked.

"Oh, I'm trying to remember an old story I used to tell a long time ago about Hoimie the Woim. All I can remember is the last line."

"You mean Herman the Worm? I know that story."

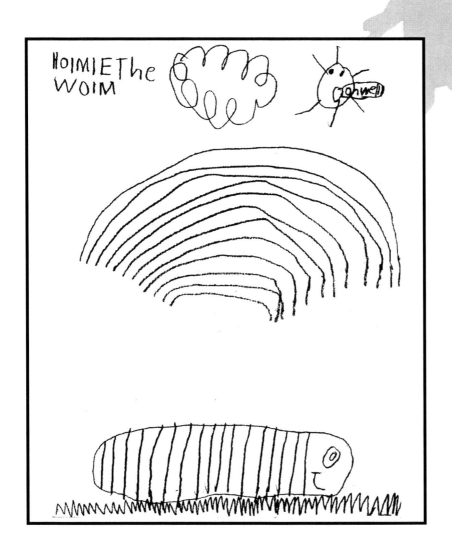

And she proceeded to tell me another version, far more fun than the one I was trying to recall. Turns out, she's the only kid in my school who knew the story that way, though some of the girls knew a version from Brownies. I made a few changes and started telling it to classes as a library warm-up story. Now that everyone knows it in my school, they're spreading it throughout New Jersey.

I have no idea where the original story started; it's part of the folk process, where stories are retold, changed, and passed around. There have always been "swallowing stories," where a not-so-nice character walks around swallowing everyone in his path until he explodes.

My other favorite story-within-a-story comes from Kathy Kim, my wonderful former editor at *Instructor* magazine. She came out to my school one May to get a firsthand look at what happens in a school library. I was warming up a class of second graders with "Hoimie the Woim," and she sat there looking puzzled. Midway through the story, I saw her turn to the teacher, Loretta Ark, and whisper, "Excuse me. What's a woim?"

"She means worm," Loretta told her.

"Ohhhh."

Some of the kids wonder what a woim is too, the first time they hear it, but someone always figures it out in the context of the story and fills them in. We then have fun talking about regional accents, such as those in Brooklyn and parts of New Joisey, Bahston, Tixas, Tinnassee, and Chicahgo.

Children's Books to Use with "Hoimie the Woim"

SEE OTHER FOOD-RELATED BOOKS LISTED UNDER "WHO THREW THE OVERALLS IN MRS. MURPHY'S CHOWDER?" PAGE 104.

Galdone, Paul. *The Greedy Old Fat Man: An American Folktale.* Illus. by the author. Clarion, 1983. (ISBN 0-89919-188-6; unp.; Grades PreK–2)

In this cumulative "swallowing" folktale, a gargantuan-bellied old man eats a hundred biscuits, a barrel of milk, a little boy and girl, a dog, a cat, a fox, and some rabbits before he is outsmarted by a squirrel.

Karas, G. Brian. *I Know an Old Lady.* Illus. by the author. Scholastic, 1994. (ISBN 0-590-46575-9; unp.; Grades PreK–2)

Try everyone's favorite swallowing song about the gluttonous old gal who swallows a horse to catch the cow, goat, dog, cat, bird, spider, and fly she just gobbled down.

Kent, Jack. *The Fat Cat: A Danish Folktale.* Illus. by the author. Parents, 1971. (ISBN 0-590-02174-5; unp.; Grades PreK–2)

Looking after an old woman's pot of gruel, a greedy cat eats the gruel, the pot, the old woman, and more in this easy-to-read swallowing story.

Kesey, Ken. *Little Tricker the Squirrel Meets Big Double the Bear.* Illus. by Barry Moser. Viking, 1990. (ISBN 0-670-81136-X; unp.; Grades 1–4)

Ravenous Big Double barrels into Topple's Bottom and swallows several animal resi-

dents until he is outsmarted by a wily red squirrel who claims he can fly.

Noble, Trinka Hakes. *The Day Jimmy's Boa Ate the Wash.* Illus. by Steven Kellogg. Dial, 1980. (ISBN 0-8037-1724-5; unp.; Grades 1–3)

Starting at the end and working backward, a boy tells his mother about his class trip to the farm, where classmate Jimmy took his giant pet snake and created chaos among the farm animals.

Polette, Nancy. *The Little Old Woman and the Hungry Cat.* Illus. by Frank Modell. Greenwillow, 1989. (ISBN 0-688-08315-3; unp.; Grades PreK–2)

The old woman's unrepentant, fat, gray-and-white cat slip, slop, slurps down 16 cupcakes, a one-legged man, a squealing pig, a wedding procession, and, to top it off, the old woman herself.

Rockwell, Thomas. *How to Eat Fried Worms.* Illus. by Emily Arnold McCully. Franklin Watts, 1973. (ISBN 0-531-02631-0; 116p.; Grades 3–6)

To win a $50 bet, Billy agrees to eat one large worm a day for 15 days.

Roth, Susan. *The Biggest Frog in Australia.* Illus. by the author. Simon & Schuster, 1996. (ISBN 0-689-80490-3; unp.; Grades PreK–2)

Back in the Dreamtime, the biggest frog was so thirsty that he drank up all the water in the puddles, billabongs, ocean, sky, and clouds, leaving the other animals to think of a scheme to make him laugh so the water could spill back out of his mouth.

Scieszka, Jon. *The True Story of the Three Little Pigs.* Illus. by Lane Smith. Viking, 1989. (ISBN 0-670-82759-2; unp.; Grades 1–6)

Alexander T. Wolf ("You can call me Al") reveals what he claims is the real story of the Three Little Pigs, insisting he was just trying to borrow a cup of sugar from the pigs for his dear old granny's birthday cake when he sneezed and knocked down their houses by accident.

Van Laan, Nancy. *The Big Fat Worm.* Illus. by Marisabina Russo. Knopf, 1987. (ISBN 0-394-88763-8; unp.; Grades PreK–1)

A big, fat bird threatens to eat a big, fat worm and is in turn bothered by a big, fat cat who is pestered by a big, fat dog, and the circle begins all over again.

Cecil Was a Caterpillar

Adapted and retold by Judy Freeman, ©1996
Thanks to Cynthia Prince, third-grade teacher in Cairo, Georgia, who heard this told
at a workshop presented by several teachers from England and then passed it on to
me. Hold your hands farther and farther apart as Cecil increases in size.
Grade Level: K–5

Cecil was a caterpillar. Cecil was MY friend.

The first time I saw Cecil, he was THIS BIG. *(Fingers half an inch apart)*

I said, "Cecil! What have you done?"

He said, "I ate all the cabbages in *Bridgewater.*"

Cecil was a caterpillar. Cecil was MY friend.

The next time I saw Cecil, he was THIS BIG.

I said, "Cecil! What have you done?"

He said, "I ate all the cabbages in *Somerset County.*"

Cecil was a caterpillar. Cecil was MY friend.

The next time I saw Cecil, he was THIS BIG.

I said, "Cecil! What have you done?"

He said, "I ate all the cabbages in *New Jersey.*"

Cecil was a caterpillar. Cecil was MY friend.

The next time I saw Cecil, he was THIS BIG.

I said, "Cecil! What have you done?"

He said, "I ate all the cabbages in the *United States.*"

Cecil was a caterpillar. Cecil was MY friend.

The next time I saw Cecil, he was THIS BIG.

I said, "Cecil! What have you done?"

He said, "I ate all the cabbages in *North America.*"

Cecil was a caterpillar. Cecil was MY friend.

The next time I saw Cecil, he was THIS BIG.

I said, "Cecil! What have you done?"

He said, "I ate all the cabbages in the *Northern Hemisphere.*"

Cecil was a caterpillar. Cecil was MY friend.
The next time I saw Cecil, he was THIS BIG.
I said, "Cecil! What have you done?"
He said, "I ate all the cabbages on *Earth*."

Cecil was a caterpillar. Cecil was MY friend.
The last time I saw Cecil, he was THIS BIG.
I said, "Cecil! What have you done?"
He said, "*HICCUP!*"

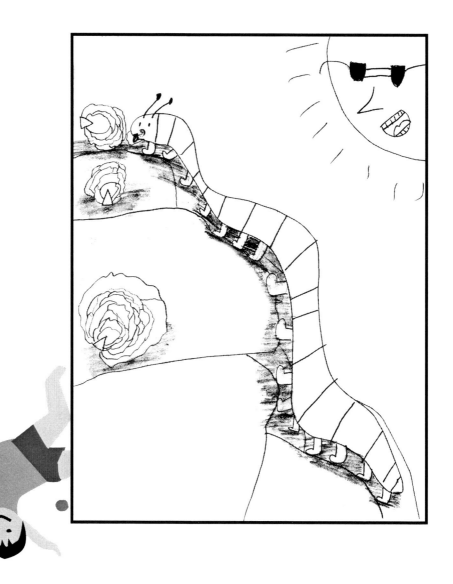

CHILDREN ENJOY PLAYING THE ADDRESS GAME: I GO TO Van Holten School, on Van Holten Road, in Bridgewater, Somerset County, New Jersey, United States, North America, Northern Hemisphere, Earth, the Solar System, the Milky Way, the Universe. While "Hoimie the Woim" is just for laughs, "Cecil" gives children the progression of their place in the universe. Change the location to fit where you are, of course, and have children draw a map of where they are.

I love songs and stories like this one, as I am prone to whip out the globe or a map with a class just to explore new places. Children need time to develop their geographical awareness, and there's no better way than to get them curious about far-flung sites introduced in stories.

Children's Books to Use with "Cecil Was a Caterpillar"

SEE ALSO FOOD-RELATED BOOKS LISTED UNDER "WHO THREW THE OVERALLS IN MRS. MURPHY'S CHOWDER?" PAGE 104.

Baer, Edith. *This Is the Way We Go to School: A Book About Children Around the World*. Illus. by Steve Björkman. Scholastic, 1990. (ISBN 0-590-43161-7; unp.; Grades K–2)

Rhyming couplets describe children from many countries as they make their way to school via roller skates, bus, the Staten Island Ferry, cable car, vaporetto, skis, and on foot.

Ball, Duncan. *Jeremy's Tail*. Illus. by Donna Rawlins. Orchard, 1991. (ISBN 0-531-08551-1; unp.; Grades PreK–2)

Determined to pin the tail on the donkey, Jeremy manages to walk onto a bus, aboard a ship, past Egyptian pyramids, across African savannahs, and, after being shot out of a cannon, back to the party again.

Bogart, Jo Ellen. *Gifts*. Illus. by Barbara Reid. Scholastic, 1996. (ISBN 0-590-55260-0; unp.; Grades PreK–2)

In a rhyme with a chantable verse, a young girl's grandmother travels the globe, asking, "What would you have me bring?" as she visits far-flung sites from China and

Australia to the Arctic, collecting souvenirs as she goes.

Brisson, Pat. *Magic Carpet*. Illus. by Amy Schwartz. Bradbury, 1991. (ISBN 0-02-714340-6; unp.; Grades 1–3)

Elizabeth plays an atlas game with her Aunt Agatha in which they sit on a small Chinese carpet and make up a story about how the rug was conveyed from China to Alaska, across the United States by truck, ending up at Agatha's house in New Jersey.

Brown, Ruth. *If At First You Do Not See*. Illus. by the author. Holt, 1983. (ISBN 0-8050-1053-X; unp.; Grades PreK–2)

A bored caterpillar nibbles his way around each page. Each sight he sees is transformed into something entirely different when the page is turned upside down.

Bursik, Rose. *Amelia's Fantastic Flight*. Illus. by the author. Henry Holt, 1992. (ISBN 0-8050-1872-7; unp.; Grades K–3)

Take an alliterative world tour with Amelia as she flies her plane on a six-continent, 14-country spin—note the map insets on each page and the full-page map of her route at the back of the book—before landing back in the United States just in time for dinner.

Carle, Eric. *The Very Hungry Caterpillar.* Illus. by the author. World, 1969. (ISBN 0-399-20853-4; unp.; Grades PreK–1)

The little fellow eats his way through the week and through each page of the book as he scarfs down fruit and a load of junk food before he builds a cocoon and becomes a butterfly.

Cherry, Lynne. *The Armadillo from Amarillo.* Illus. by the author. Harcourt, 1994. (ISBN 0-15-200359-2; unp.; Grades 1–4)

Wondering what's beyond his woods, Texas armadillo Sasparillo travels cross-country and by eagle-back to see the country, continent, and even the earth from space.

Clements, Andrew. *Mother Earth's Counting Book.* Illus. by Lonni Sue Johnson. Picture Book Studio, 1992. (ISBN 0-88708-138-X; unp.; Grades K–2)

Count to ten and back again with an appealing introduction to the planet featuring 1 earth, 2 poles, 3 climate zones, 4 oceans, plus assorted landforms and animals that will provide a thoughtful introduction to a geography and globe unit.

Heiligman, Deborah. *From Caterpillar to Butterfly.* Illus. by Bari Weissman. HarperCollins, 1996. (ISBN 0-06-024268-X; 32p.; Grades K–2)

In a colorful nonfiction picture book from the Let's-Read-and-Find-Out Science series, we follow the metamorphosis of a caterpillar into a painted-lady butterfly.

Lobel, Anita. *Away from Home.* Illus. by the author. Greenwillow, 1994. (ISBN 0-688-10355-3; unp.; Grades K–2)

An alphabetical cast of 26 boys act out one tableau each, highlighting an alliterative city, such as, "Lloyd limped in London." Children can write and illustrate new action sentences using their own names and other places around the globe.

McBratney, Sam. *The Caterpillow Fight.* Illus. by Jill Barton. Candlewick, 1996. (ISBN 1-56402-804-6; unp.; Grades PreK–2)

In the middle of the night seven caterpillars have a rousing pillow fight until feathers fly.

Priceman, Marjorie. *How to Make an Apple Pie and See the World.* Illus. by the author. Knopf, 1994. (ISBN 0-679-93705-6; unp.; Grades K–2)

If the market's closed, you'll need to travel the globe to get the ingredients, as the heroine of this how-to guide demonstrates. There's an apple pie recipe appended, just in case you and your kids feel ambitious.

Sheldon, Dyan. *Love, Your Bear Pete.* Illus. by Tania Hurt-Newton. Candlewick, 1994. (ISBN 1-56402-332-X; unp.; Grades K–2)

Left by mistake on the bus, Brenda's light-blue teddy bear sends her postcards from all the places he's off visiting: London, Paris, Venice, and around the world, until he returns to her in the mail.

Singer, Marilyn. *Nine O'Clock Lullaby.* Illus. by Frané Lessac. HarperCollins, 1991. (ISBN 0-06-025648-6; unp.; Grades K–2)

When it's 9 P.M. in Brooklyn, New York, it's 10 P.M. in Puerto Rico, midnight on the mid-Atlantic Ocean, and, as we circumnavigate the globe to visit other countries, we see what others are doing as we get ready for bed.

Wells, Robert E. *Is a Blue Whale the Biggest Thing There Is?* Illus. by the author. Albert Whitman, 1993. (ISBN 0-8075-3655-5; unp.; Grades 2–5)

Compare the relative size of whales to Mount Everest, to the earth, to the sun, to a supergiant star, to the Milky Way, and to the universe, which is, finally, the biggest thing there is.

Henry My Son

Grade Level: K–3

Where have you been all the day, Henry my son?
Where have you been all the day, my little one?
In the woods, dear mother, in the woods, dear mother;
Mother be quick, I've got to be sick, and lay me down to die.

What did you do in the woods all day, Henry my son?
What did you do in the woods all day, my little one?
Ate, dear mother, ate, dear mother;
Mother be quick, I've got to be sick, and lay me down to die.

What did you eat in the woods all day, Henry my son?
What did you eat in the woods all day, my little one?
Eels, dear mother, eels, dear mother;
Mother be quick, I've got to be sick, and lay me down to die.

What color was those eels, Henry my son?
What color was those eels, my little one?
Green and yeller, green and yeller;
Mother be quick, I've got to be sick, and lay me down to die.

Those eels was snakes, Henry my son.
Those eels was snakes, my little one.
Ohhhh, dear mother, ohhhh, dear mother;
Mother be quick, I've got to be sick, and lay me down to die.

What color flowers would you like, Henry my son?
What color flowers would you like, my little one?
Green and yeller, green and yeller;
Mother be quick, I've got to be sick, and lay me down to die.

Henry My Son

Traditional

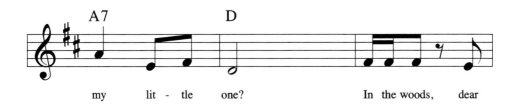

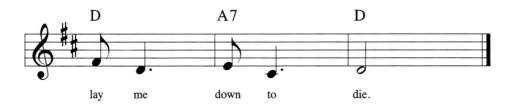

I LEARNED THIS SONG, A CHILDREN'S VERSION OF THE OLD English ballad "Lord Randall," from Pete Seeger's "Children's Concert at Town Hall," a record I've had since childhood and still treasure.

Sing this song once, and have your listeners join in on the "Mother be quick" refrain. The next time through, ask them to retell the sequence and sing each verse with you. Point out that the grammar is not quite proper, it being country talk, and explain to those with eyebrows raised that yes, "yeller" does mean yellow. Be sure to ask why his mother inquires about his preference in flowers. "It's for his grave," someone is sure to contribute, though I assure listeners that even if Henry had a whopper of a bellyache, he was probably fine after he had a bit of a lie-down.

Act the story out in pairs, with half of the kids playing Henry and the other half playing the questioning parent. Gummy worms in the obvious colors would make an ideal follow-up treat.

Children's Books to Use with "Henry My Son"

SEE ALSO FOOD-RELATED BOOKS LISTED UNDER "WHO THREW THE OVERALLS IN MRS. MURPHY'S CHOWDER?" PAGE 104.

Bodsworth, Nan. *A Nice Walk in the Jungle.* Illus. by the author. Viking Kestrel, 1989. (ISBN 0-670-82476-3; unp.; Grades K–2)

On a class walk through the jungle, only teacher Miss Jellaby, intent on pointing out exciting nature scenes, seems unaware that a boa constrictor is eating all the children, one by one.

Charlip, Remy, and Burton Supree. *Mother, Mother, I Feel Sick, Send for the Doctor Quick, Quick, Quick.* Illus. by Remy Charlip. Buccaneer, 1993. (ISBN 1-56849-172-7; unp.; Grades K–2)

A boy has swallowed apples, a ball, a birthday cake, spaghetti, and far more, as we view the silhouetted operation to remove everything from his belly in this rhyming shadow play.

Cherry, Lynne. *Who's Sick Today?* Illus. by the author. Dutton, 1988. (ISBN 0-525-44380-0; unp.; Grades K–2)

There are beavers with fevers, a snake with an ache, and a wardful of other ailing animals. Children love to add new patients to the infirmary by making up new rhymes and illustrating them.

Czernecki, Stefan, and Timothy Rhodes. *The Singing Snake.* Illus. by Stefan Czernecki. Hyperion, 1993. (ISBN 1-56282-400-7; unp.; Grades K–2)

In this pourquoi tale about the first flute and how snakes got their hiss, Old Man promises to make a musical instrument to honor the creature that sings the best, and Snake wins by cheating.

Davol, Marguerite W. *How Snake Got His Hiss: An Original Tale*. Illus. by Mercedes McDonald. Orchard, 1996. (ISBN 0-531-08768-9; unp.; Grades PreK–2)

Here's a humorous pourquoi tale that explains how snakes came to look and sound the way they do today, thanks to self-important Snake, who puffs himself up and rolls along, paying no attention to the other animals in his path.

Loomis, Christine. *One Cow Coughs: A Counting Book for the Sick and Miserable*. Illus. by Pat Dypold. Ticknor & Fields, 1994. (ISBN 0-395-67899-4; unp.; Grades PreK–2)

One cow coughs, two mules moan, three sheep shake, on up to ten, and then we count back to one to find out how each set of farm animals remedies its illness.

MacDonald, Amy. *Rachel Fister's Blister*. Illus. by Marjorie Priceman. Houghton Mifflin, 1990. (ISBN 0-395-52152-1; unp.; Grades K–2)

What a rhyming to-do ensues when young Rachel finds a blister on her left-hand little toe, sending everyone into a tizzy wondering how to fix it, until they summon level-headed Queen Alice.

Nash, Ogden. *The Adventures of Isabel*. Illus. by James Marshall. Little, Brown, 1991. (ISBN 0-316-59874-7; unp.; Grades 2–5)

In a complete version of Nash's comical poem, illustrated with Marshall's uproarious watercolors, meet red-headed kid Isabel and see how a hungry bear, a wicked witch, a hideous giant, a troublesome doctor, and a horrible dream all learn the hard way not to mess with her.

Mrs. Murphy's Chowder

A Bibliography of Children's Songbooks and Resources

You'll want to consider the following standards in the field if you're looking for additional marvelous resources to beef up your library's song collection and keep kids humming.

Baltuck, Naomi. *Crazy Gibberish and Other Story Hour Stretches* (*From a Storyteller's Bag of Tricks*). Illus. by Doug Cushman. Linnett, 1993. (ISBN 0-208-02336-4; 152p.; Grades PreK–6)

An audiocassette is also available with this book, a gathering of truly wonderful songs, stories, and then some.

Delamar, Gloria T., comp. *Children's Counting-Out Rhymes, Fingerplays, Jump-Rope and Bounce-Ball Chants and Other Rhythms: A Comprehensive English Language Reference*. McFarland, 1983. (ISBN 0-89950-064-1; 206p.; Grades PreK–5)

Although this book set out to be an adult reference, with a dull cover to prove it, the sheer wealth of nonsense within is too good to keep away from the kids.

Fox, Dan, ed. *Go In and Out the Window: An Illustrated Songbook for Young People*. Henry Holt, 1987. (ISBN 0-8050-0628-1; 144p.; Grades PreK–6)

There are 61 familiar folksongs in this gorgeous collection, each accompanied by color reproductions of artwork from the Metropolitan Museum of Art in New York.

Freeman, Judy. *Books Kids Will Sit Still For: The Complete Read-Aloud Guide*. R. R. Bowker, 1990. (ISBN 0-8352-3013-4; 660p.; Professional)

An annotated bibliography of more than 2,100 children's books to read aloud to grades PreK-6, plus a text offering practical advice on booktalking, storytelling, creative drama, and literature-based activities.

Freeman, Judy. *More Books Kids Will Sit Still For*. R. R. Bowker, 1995. (ISBN 0-8352-3520-3; 869p.; Professional)

An all-new text expounds on developing book selection skills, read-aloud tricks and techniques, and down-to-earth ways to nurture an exemplary school library program, along with an annotated bibliography of more than 1,400 additional children's books to read aloud for grades PreK-6.

Garson, Eugenia, ed. *The Laura Ingalls Wilder Songbook: Favorite Songs from the Little House*. Illus. by Garth Williams. HarperCollins, 1996. (ISBN 0-06-027036-5; 160p.; Grades 2–5)

The 62 songs in this handsome collection include the score, chords, and lyrics to ballads, patriotic songs, love songs, and others from Wilder's beloved books.

Glazer, Tom, comp. *Tom Glazer's Treasury of Songs for Children*. Illus. by John O'Brien. Doubleday, 1988. (ISBN 0-385-23693-X; 256p.; Grades PreK–6)

Originally published by Grossett in 1964 as *Tom Glazer's Treasury of Folk Songs*, this updated and newly illustrated version contains more than 100 popular folk songs for every occasion.

Hart, Jane, comp. *Singing Bee! A Collection of Favorite Children's Songs*. Illus. by Anita Lobel. Lothrop, 1982. (ISBN 0-688-41975-5; 160p.; Grades K–2)

Each of the 125 well-known songs is accompanied by music, chords, and soft, beautiful illustrations.

Krull, Kathleen, comp. *Gonna Sing My Head Off! American Folk Songs for Children*. Illus. by Allen Garns. Knopf, 1992. (ISBN 0-394-81991-8; 146p.; Grades K–5)

More than 60 stellar folk songs with music, chords, and colorful pastel illustrations will provide tunes for every occasion.

Mattox, Cheryl, comp. *Shake It to the One That You Love the Best: Play Songs and Lullabies from Black Musical Traditions*. Illus. by Varnette P. Honeywood and Brenda Joysmith. Warren-Mattox Productions, 1989. (ISBN 0-9623381-0-9; unp.; Grades PreK–2)

The 26 spirited songs and chants in this vibrantly illustrated songbook provide music and notes for accompanying games.

Nelson, Esther L. *The Funny Songbook*. Illus. by Joyce Behr. Sterling, 1984. (ISBN 0-8069-4682-2; 96p.; Grades PreK–6)

This is a necessary item in anyone's silly-song collection, along with *The Fun-to-Sing Songbook* (1986) and *The Silly Song Book* (1981).

Raffi. *The Raffi Singable Songbook: A Collection of 51 Songs from Raffi's First Three Records for Very Young Children*. Illus. by Joyce Yamomoto. Crown, 1987. (ISBN 0-517-56638-9; 106p.; Grades PreK–2)

Singers will appreciate this useful companion to the first three Raffi records, along with *The Second Raffi Songbook* (1986).

Seeger, Ruth Crawford, comp. *American Folk Songs for Children*. Illus. by Barbara Cooney. Doubleday, 1980. (ISBN 0-385-15788-6; 190p.; Grades PreK–4)

A classic in the field of children's songs; Seeger's suggestions for play, games, and improvisations remain right on target.

Tashjian, Virginia, ed. *Juba This & Juba That: Favorite Children's Songs to Sing, Stories to Tell, Rhymes to Chant, Riddles to Guess & More*. Second ed. Illus. by Nadine Bernard Westcott. Little, Brown, 1995. (ISBN 0-316-83234-0; 116p.; Grades PreK–4)

Kids love this book, and beginning storytellers and music lovers will find it and its companion, *With a Deep Sea Smile* (1974), indispensable sources of easy-to-learn material.

Weiss, Nicki, sel. *If You're Happy and You Know It: Eighteen Story Songs Set to Pictures*. Illus. by the author. Greenwillow, 1987. (ISBN 0-688-06444-2; 40p., Grades PreK–2)

The best feature of this attractive songbook is that children can read each song themselves.

Winn, Marie, comp. *The Fireside Book of Fun and Game Songs*. Illus. by Whitney Darrow, Jr. Simon & Schuster, 1974. (ISBN 0-671-65213-3; 222p.; Grades PreK–6)

The grandmommy of great silly-song books, this one includes some of the best.

Index of Authors, Titles, and Subjects

This index gives access by author, by title, and by subject. Authors' names are inverted; titles of books are in italics followed by author name in parentheses; titles of songs, chants, and stories are in quotation marks and followed by the word (SONG); subject headings are in capital letters.

M

McBratney, Sam. *The Caterpillow Fight*, 118

McBroom Tells the Truth (Fleischman, Sid), 6, 40

McCoy, Karen Kawamoto. *A Tale of Two Tengu: A Japanese Folktale*, 44

MacDonald, Amy. *Rachel Fister's Blister*, 123

McGovern, Ann. *Drop Everything, It's D.E.A.R. Time!*, 14

McPhail, David.
  Fix-It, 14
  Lost!, 14
  Santa's Book of Names, 14

Magic Carpet (Brisson, Pat), 117

Mama Don't Allow (Hurd, Thacher), 99

Marshall, James.
  Old Mother Hubbard and Her Wonderful Dog, 54
  Wings: A Tale of Two Chickens, 25, 85

Marshall, James, comp. *James Marshall's Mother Goose*, 54

Mathews, Louise. *Gator Pie*, 99

Mattox, Cheryl, comp. *Shake It to the One That You Love the Best*, 126

Melvil and Dewey in the Chips (Swallow, Pam), 25

Michael Foreman's Mother Goose (Foreman, Michael, comp.), 53

Minters, Frances. *Cinder-Elly*, 58

Misoso: Once Upon a Time Tales from Africa (Aardema, Verna), 45

Moon Rope: Un Lazo a la Luna: A Peruvian Folktale (Ehlert, Lois), 45

More Books Kids Will Sit Still For (Freeman, Judy), 44, 125

More Than Anything Else (Bradby, Marie), 32

Moss Gown (Hooks, William), 45

The Most Wonderful Egg in the World (Heine, Helme), 84

Most, Bernard. *Zoodles*, 90

Mother Earth's Counting Book (Clements, Andrew), 118

The Mother Goose Songbook (Glazer, Tom, comp.), 54

Mother, Mother, I Feel Sick, Send for the Doctor Quick, Quick, Quick (Charlip, Remy, and Burton Supree), 122

MOTHERS, 63

MOTHERS AND SONS, 60–61, 119–120

"Mrs. Murphy's Chowder" (SONG), 105–107

Munching: Poems about Eating (Hopkins, Lee Bennett, comp.), 104

"My Father Shot a Kangaroo" (SONG), 78–79

"My Tall Silk Hat" (SONG), 66–69

My Tang's Tungled and Other Ridiculous Situations (Brewton, Sara, John E. Brewton, and G. Meredith Blackburn, III, comps.), 89

My Very First Mother Goose (Opie, Iona, ed.), 54

Myers, Bernice. *Sidney Rella and the Glass Sneaker*, 58

N

Nash, Ogden. *The Adventures of Isabel*, 123

Nelson, Esther L. *The Funny Songbook*, 126

Never Kiss an Alligator! (Bare, Colleen Stanley), 98

Never Take a Pig to Lunch and Other Poems About the Fun of Eating (Westcott, Nadine Bernard, sel.), 104

A Nice Walk in the Jungle (Bodsworth, Nan), 122

Nine O'Clock Lullaby (Singer, Marilyn), 118

Nixon, Joan Lowery. *If You Were a Writer*, 25

Noble, Trinka Hakes. *The Day Jimmy's Boa Ate the Wash*, 113

NONSENSE VERSES, 60–61, 64–65, 72–74, , 76–79, 82–83, 86–92

Novak, Matt. *Gertie and Gumbo*, 99

NURSERY RHYMES, 51–54

O

"Ode to Nonfiction" (SONG), 18–19

"Oh I Had a Little Chicken / I Went to Cincinnati" (SONG), 7, 82–83

Oh, Such Foolishness! (Cole, William, comp.), 89

Old Mother Hubbard and Her Wonderful Dog (Marshall, James), 54

Olive and the Magic Hat (Christelow, Eileen), 70

Once Inside the Library (Huff, Barbara A.), 24

"One Bright Day" (SONG), 65

One Cow Coughs: A Counting Book for the Sick and Miserable (Loomis, Christine), 123

Opie, Iona, ed. *My Very First Mother Goose*, 54

Opie, Iona, and Peter Opie, eds.
  I Saw Esau: The Schoolchild's Pocket Book, 90
  Tail Feathers from Mother Goose: The Opie Rhyme Book, 54

Opie, Peter, jt. ed.
  I Saw Esau: The Schoolchild's Pocket Book, 90
  Tail Feathers from Mother Goose: The Opie Rhyme Book, 54

The Orchard Book of Nursery Rhymes (Sutherland, Zena, comp.), 54

The Ordinary Princess (Kaye, M. M.), 58

P

Palatini, Margie. *Piggie Pie*, 99

Papa Gatto: An Italian Fairy Tale (Sanderson, Ruth), 45

PARODIES, 51–54, 55–59

PARTS OF A BOOK, 12–13, 21–23

Peeping Beauty (Auch, Mary Jane), 84

Petunia (DuVoisin, Roger), 14

Phillips, Louis. *263 Brain Busters: Just How Smart Are You, Anyway?*, 90

Piggie Pie (Palatini, Margie), 99

Pinkwater, Daniel. *The Hoboken Chicken Emergency*, 85

Poem Stew (Cole, William, comp.), 104

Poems of A. Nonny Mouse (Prelutsky, Jack, comp.), 90